T

THE COMMUNIST CHOICE

Understanding the Present
Changing the Future

Science éditions Marxiste

Marxist Science Publications

For information about our publications please contact
Éditions Science Marxiste S.A.R.L.
10, rue Lavoisier – 93100 Montreuil-sous-Bois, France
E-mail: escmrx@wanadoo.fr – Fax : (+) 33 1 49 88 79 82
http://www.sciencemarxiste.com

ISSN 1772-4511
ISBN 978-2-912639-37-0

Publisher's note

This edition is a complete translation of the "La Scelta Comunista" ed. Lotta Comunista November 2008.
This translation is based on the original Italian.

«... the function of the revolutionary party is not, and cannot be, merely that of "prediction". Marxism provides us with the analytical tools to identify and "predict" the tendencies of capitalist development - its conflicts, its contradictions, its afflictions: this is why Marxism is a science. But for revolutionaries "prediction" is only the necessary condition of political action, of political struggle: this is why Marxism is above all the science of revolution, the science of the relationship between objective circumstances, historically determined, and the subjective and conscious intervention of the Party».

Arrigo Cervetto, 1969

Index

A life choice for freedom

«...these replies are intended for practical use (...)
to be torn from the "narrow walls of intellectuals' studies"
and to address those (...)
for whom "ideals" are necessary,
because without ideals they cannot live well ».

Lenin, 1894

Today, understanding reality is more important than ever. Our "*global*" society is characterised by crucial changes that come about even if we do not understand them, while history is *accelerating* in an extraordinary way: in the space of a few years, the greatest world power – the USA – has witnessed its own sharp decline, and, in the midst of a global crisis, seems to be the weakest point: new powers – China and India, to name only the principals – are developing at an extraordinary pace, involving over a third of the human race: European countries that took part in the most savage bloodbaths of the last century are unifying in order to resist competition from the new powers.

The world of finance is being continually shaken by crises that strike at millions of people: apart from the open sore of Iraq, dozens of other conflicts are staining the world with blood, while the FAO (the United Nations' Food and Agricultural Organisation) announces that because of the current food crisis, an additional one hundred million people will slip from a condition of being underfed to a level of malnutrition, bringing to one-sixth the proportion of humanity suffering from starvation.

The picture before us is of a rapidly changing world, in which the emerging powers are starting to claim the elbow room owed them by virtue of their increased power: a world in which the declining powers are preparing to fight to retain their privileges, while a general economic interdependence frequently rewards the political actions of governments with *unintended results*.

To fail to understand the dialectic of the events that are dominating the world is to be impotent witnesses, or victims, of these events.

The great lies of the last century have been laid low: first and foremost the lie that there existed countries in which socialism, the society of the future, had been achieved. Ideologies, like Nature, abhor a vacuum. The ruling class is testing the strength of powerful new ideas, trying to sell religion, and Catholicism in particular.

«*A conservative and reactionary ideology, but one based on a strong and efficient organisation, and able to exploit the experience of centuries. An ideology that a greedy and cynical bourgeoisie needs to fill its ideological vacuum and to soothe its glaring sores*».[1]

As Marxists, we have not forgotten that it was the Encyclopedist Diderot – one of the greatest intellectuals of the bourgeoisie at the time of its revolutionary phase – who wrote: «*Lost by night in an immense forest, I have nothing but a little lantern to guide me. A stranger comes along and says: "My friend, a better way to find your path would be to blow out the flame". The stranger is a theologian*».

We are searching for young people who *don't want to blow out the flame*, who have the *courage* as well as the *taste* for the struggle, in a world that stands at the threshold of epochal upheavals: young people able to reject myths and illusions, in order to be the heroes of their own lives.

Today the bourgeoisie carefully selects and moulds its own leading cadres, but when it speaks to the great mass of youth it is reduced to defending disengagement, sometimes going so far as to pass off as freedom choices involving degradation and subjection, such as the use of drugs. This is not to moralise the issue, but the game we have to play requires a clear attitude of *zero tolerance*: those who set out to change the world need all the lucidity, strength and intelligence with which Nature has endowed them.

There are young people like this in every generation: perceptive young people who are not content with the prepackaged replies of *common sense*, who want to take part in the age-old struggle between the defenders of privilege and those who instead interpret the common interests of the human species.

This struggle, which runs through the whole of human history, today sees the bourgeoisie, who rule by « *submerging everything in the icy waters of self-serving calculation* » – as Marx and Engels write in the *Manifesto* – opposing the Communists, who fight « *to give to everyone according to their needs* ».

From the barricades of the Paris Commune to the October Revolution to the thousands of battles fought by the workers over two centuries and throughout the world, in the vanguard of the struggle there have always been groups of young people who have been both inspiration and guide, and who have left their mark on history.

Today, that struggle is at a crucial turning point. And the potential field strength in this battle is immense. According to World Bank estimates, young people between 15 and 24 make up 18 % of the world population – around 1,200,000,000 individuals. They differ in terms of social conditions, culture, language and life expectancy, but they are united by factors other than their chronological age.

For the 60 million young people who live there, the metropolises of Europe are an opulent oasis in the midst of a world situation in which hunger is not merely a spectre from the past.

In Europe, a large proportion of young people are still in the world of school: a very high percentage receive primary and secondary level education, and in a number of countries, such as France and Italy, 60 % of the relevant age group go to university.

But this situation of relative well-being does not cancel out the state of uncertainty bred by the imperialist age in which we live. The young who enter the job market as hands and brains for the production of surplus value encounter millions of immigrants, to whom they are linked by a common condition: exploitation. All belong to the only international class whose historic destiny is to overthrow existing bourgeois society. The young immigrants can expect to occupy only the lowest rungs of the social ladder: a study from the Milan Chamber of Commerce found that over a period of three years the number of immigrant nursing staff in the metropolis had tripled, while in many factories in the north of Italy all the workers with the lowest qualifications are immigrants. This holds true for the whole of Europe: France takes in 200,000 immigrants every year: in Great Britain they represent 10 % of the population: in Germany 13 % in the seven years from 2001 to 2006: one and a half million have entered Spain from Latin America alone.

« *"The number and the misery of the proletariat increase continuously". This is incorrect when put in such a categorical way. The organisation of the workers, and their constantly growing resistance, will possibly check the increase of misery to a certain extent. However, what certainly does increase is the insecurity of existence. I should insert this* ».[2]

This was Engel's precise definition, as early as 1891, correcting those German Social Democrats who spoke of the spread of poverty.

If we widen our perspective to include the world, we realise how *the uncertainty of existence* is precisely the common element of the *young generations* of all continents. Let's be clear: for a great number of individuals born on Earth, the biggest problem is still *managing* to have a period of youth.

According to the 2008 UNICEF report, in the world today nearly 10 million children under the age of five die every year: around two thousand have died since you began to read this book. Almost all these deaths could be avoided by modest financial intervention: prevention consists of vaccination, use of mosquito nets, and administering a solution of water and mineral salts. But in a world which during 2007 threw away 1,204 billion dollars on military spending, such resources cannot be found, to the extent that the terms *ambitious* and *extraordinary effort* can be applied to a project that aims to reduce mortality figures for under-fives to *only* 9,000 deaths per day by 2015 – for what such projects are worth, given the frequency with which they fail to get off the ground.

Not to speak of the many children under the age of 15 who are used as soldiers by 24 different countries. Only recently have the dimensions of the slaughter during the Iran-Iraq war 30 years ago been ascertained: when groups of young boys were herded in front of the advancing troops, to sacrifice their lives in clearing the way of land mines. According to the standing tribunal on crimes against humanity, set up by an international treaty ratified by 106 different states (missing from the roll call are important states such as the USA and China) the number of children who today still form part of military bodies is as high as 300,000, in spite of the ban approved by ONU in 2000. Extreme cases, but real people who have had their childhoods, and often their lives, stolen by imperialist wars: extreme cases to which, in a cynical and brutal world, we cannot remain indifferent. Not charity, nor humanitarian good intentions, – still less the *standing tribunals* set up by those same imperialist countries that produce and sell arms – can change this: on the contrary, all this can only relieve the world's conscience, or turn the spotlight on some Hollywood star in search of easy popularity.

We know exactly how the crises and the wars that are so much a part of our world depend on the mechanisms by which our society works, and not on human bad faith, nor on the malign intentions of politicians: and how the future of this particular current social system must inevitably be marked by violent and bloody conflict. It is with this that the young proletariat have to reckon, because it will be down to them to face the struggle with a ruling class disposed to every atrocity so as not to lose its grip on power. The age of *war and revolution* that opened with the First World War and with the October Revolution continues: capitalist development and the birth of new imperialist powers will lead to a new turning-point.

The last twenty years have transformed the world in which we live. When the Berlin Wall fell, and the old lie of socialism in Russia and in Europe vanished, the intellectuals of the ruling class told us that at last there would be peace in the world, and that a new era of co-operation was opening up.

No sooner had the ruins of the Wall fallen, than the Gulf War (1990-1991, and over 80,000 dead) began: then came the war in the former Yugoslavia (1991-1995): then Georgia (1992-1993): Chechyna (1994-2004) and Kosovo (1999): in 2001 came the US/European imperialist invasion of Afghanistan: in 2003 the new Gulf war, which, like the series of conflicts in the former Soviet republics, is in effect not yet over. To these we can add the Middle East conflict, the sequel to the bloody African wars, and the many «*little hotbeds*» spread over the world. Millions of young people have lost their lives in the years of «*peace*» that have followed the end of the Second World War: in fact, the guns have not fallen silent for even a day during the years of capitalism's *peaceful* development. When fierce competition between the powers breaks out again, when the balance is shattered anew, how can we believe that the ruling class will draw back from yet more massacres?

This reality is not an easy thing to grasp. We are used to seeing both natural and social catastrophes on our television screens: we have become used to thinking that war, poverty and the struggle to survive are all to do with other people: that our natural condition is to be observers.

Laziness, the capacity of a rich and opulent society to corrupt us, *common sense* – all end by convincing us that disaster cannot *really* strike us: that a solution can always be found: even – a historically common intellectual attitude – that we, as individuals, will always be able to get ourselves out of a hole.

The English historian Arnold Toynbee, recalling the celebrations for the 60th anniversary of Queen Victoria's accession to the throne (five days of celebration, in the June of 1897) remembers how he – a child of eight following the parade from the shoulders of his uncle – was struck by the atmosphere of general euphoria:

«*I remember the atmosphere. It was "we head the world, we're at the top, and we'll stay there forever. Naturally, there's something called history, but history is an unpleasant thing that happens to others. And we're sure of being comfortable, and apart from all that". But of course*» goes on Faared Zakaria, who passes on this anecdote, «*history also involved Great Britain*».[3]

The First World War put a brutal end to the dream of the Belle Époque, dramatically demonstrating that to follow *common sense* results only in *being unprepared* for the future. But there is another option: to understand the reality of the society in which we live, to explain its contradictions, and to fight for something better, as exemplified by the October Revolution.

This book sets out to reply to the questions:

Is there a scientific method for understanding the reality of a society?

Can we prove its analyses?

What will happen in the world in the next few decades?

What are the tools for intervening in history?

Can we have a society in which the human race co-operates for the common good?

The worst ills of our era are not caused by Nature, nor by «*Fate*»: they arise from the way in which our society is organised, from a society in which we live divided into classes: to renounce our class, or to fight against it, is to be complicit – consciously or otherwise – with the ruling class.

Communists do not surrender to the difficulties of this struggle: they «*learned the rhythm of history, that is, the dialectics of the class struggle. They also learned [..] how to subordinate their subjective plans and programs to this objective rhythm. They learned not to fall into despair over the fact that the laws of history do not depend upon their individual tastes and are not subordinated to their own moral criteria. They learned to subordinate their individual desires to the laws of history. They learned not to become frightened by the most powerful enemies [..]. They know how to swim against the stream*».[4]

We believe that there are ideals worth fighting for: in fact, we speak to those «*for whom ideals are necessary, because without them they can't live well*»[5] but we are not naive Utopians.

We know that « *a huge amount of preparatory – and by its nature invisible – work is required* » but if the goal is clear, a young person will not be frightened of work, of consistent commitment, by the prospect of struggle.

The ruling class is preparing for us a future of war and barbarism: Communism offers us the solid possibility of a world in which: « *after the enslaving subordination of the individual to the division of labour, and therewith also the antithesis between mental and physical labour, has vanished: after labour has become not only a means of life, but life's prime want: after the productive forces have also increased, with the all-round development of the individual, and all the springs of co-operative wealth flow more abundantly – only then can the narrow horizon of bourgeois right be crossed in its entirety, and society inscribe on its banners: From each according to his ability: to each according to his need!* »[6]

Chapter One

Marxism: a guide for action

"Nature is grand, but history seems grander to me than nature. Nature has taken millions of years to generate conscious beings, and these conscious beings now need thousands of years to act consciously together – that is, with the consciousness not only of their actions as individuals, but also of their actions as a mass – cooperating and pursuing a common goal that was chosen in advance. We have almost reached this situation. Observing this process, the approaching of something that has never existed before in our Earth's history, I see a show worth watching. Throughout my entire life I have never been able to take my eyes off it."

Friedrich Engels, 1893
(*Letter to George William Lamplugh*,
quoted in Arrigo Cervetto's
"The Difficult Question Of Times"
Marxist Science Publications 2003 Page 75)

In his autobiography, Albert Einstein writes that at the age of only twelve he became convinced that much of what was being conveyed to him by the *traditional educational machine* simply *could not be true,* and that it was this awareness that prompted him towards free thinking and scientific research.

In the same spirit, around fifty years previously, after having dedicated himself passionately to the study of law, philosophy and history, the young Marx had become persuaded of the falsity of the dominant view, according to which human history was determined by the conflict of ideas. He had therefore decided to turn to the study of society with the approach of the true scientist, who refuses to be influenced by current prejudice.

In an 1859 text – from which the subsequent quotations are taken – he candidly describes the results of his studies: « *My inquiry led me to the conclusion that neither legal relations nor political forms could be comprehended either by themselves or on the basis of a so-called general development of the human mind, but that on the contrary they originate in the material conditions of life* ».[7] This, then, was the essential starting point.

In Paris, he embarks on the study of political economy, which convinces him that: « *In the social production of their existence, men inevitably enter into definite relations which are independent of their will, namely relations of production appropriate to a given stage in the development of their material forces of production* ».

The *production* of their existence, the struggle to survive in the face of the adversities of Nature, brings human beings into relations with each other: when we speak of *mode of production* we mean precisely the *way* in which our species, in a given period of history, produces the conditions for its existence. « *The totality of these relations of production constitutes the economic structure of society, the real foundation on which arises a legal and political superstructure, and to which correspond definite forms of social consciousness*».

There exists, therefore, a *fundamental* structure, which is the mode of production, and on this stands society's juridical, political and cultural superstructure: taken together, this is what distinguishes a particular *economic/social ormation.* Marxism recognises the enormous importance of the *superstructure*, which is the field for the political and ideological struggles of States and Religions, and for the ways in which the human race portrays itself and its social life: but in the final analysis, Marxism singles out the basis of the *structure* « *the mode of production of the materials of life has a widespread influence upon life's social, political and spiritual processes. It is not human consciousness that determines human existence: on the contrary, it is the human social condition that determines human consciousness*».

This is a completely new point of view. History has always been seen as the product of a struggle between antagonists – military leaders, politicians, factions – who sought to impose their *ideas*: instead, Marx discovers the laws of movement of social development by studying the various economic/social formations that have succeeded each other in the course of human history.

Lenin comments: « *The chaos and arbitrariness that had previously reigned in views on history and politics were replaced by a strikingly integral and harmonious scientific theory, which shows how, in consequence of the growth of productive forces, out of one system of social life another and higher system develops - how capitalism, for instance, grows out of feudalism*».[8]

As Darwin (Marx and Engels were among the most enthusiastic supporters of his theories) had not allowed himself to be influenced by the Creation myths – widespread and deep-rooted as these were – and by studying reality without preconceptions had discovered the laws that regulate how species are born and die out in the struggle for life, so Marx discovered that relations of production between people change, and that from this change is born the very history of humanity.

In the work quoted above, Marx continues: « *at a certain stage of development, the material productive forces of society come into conflict with the existing relations of production or – this merely expresses the same thing in legal terms – with the property relations within the framework of which they have hitherto operated* ».

« *Then begins an epoch of social revolution* » continues Marx, thus freeing the idea of revolution from any sentimentality and affirming its historical *necessity*, underlining how *class struggle* – conscious or not – is the real motor of human history. The outcome of the struggle is not guaranteed: « *oppressor and oppressed stood in constant opposition to one another, carried on an uninterrupted, now hidden, now open fight, a fight that each time ended either in a revolutionary reconstitution of society at large, or in the common ruin of the contending classes* ».[9] and this is why revolutionaries have such an important role to play in history.

From where had Marx taken the intellectual tools that had allowed him to make such an accurate analysis of human society?

In *The Three Sources and Three Component Parts of Marxism*, published in March 1913 and dedicated to the thirtieth anniversary of the death of Marx, Lenin underlines how the genius of Marxist theory lies in having resolved a series of problems posed by the vanguard of human thought by placing itself in direct and unbroken line from the doctrines of the greatest representatives of philosophy, political economy and socialism: German philosophy, British political economy, and French socialism. From a philosophical point of view, the basis of Marxism is materialism, even if: « *Marx did not stop at eighteenth-century materialism; he developed philosophy to a higher level, he enriched it with the achievements of German classical philosophy, especially of Hegel's system, which in its turn had led to the materialism of Feuerbach. The main achievement was* dialectics *i.e. the doctrine of development in its fullest, deepest and most comprehensive form, the doctrine of the relativity of human knowledge that provides us with a reflection of eternally developing matter* ».[10] The second source of Marxism is classical political economy which, born in Great Britain (the most advanced country of the time) with the studies of Adam Smith and David Ricardo, had already arrived at the theory according to which value derives from labour: «*Marx* continued *their work; he provided a proof of the theory and developed it consistently*».

From this point of departure, Marx studies the mechanisms by which capitalism functions, explains scientifically the concept of exploitation of the working class, demonstrating how a part of the value produced by this class is expropriated, affirms the transitory nature of the mode of capitalist production, and identifies the proletariat as the future author of the new *social revolution.*

Furthermore, Marx returns to the concept of history as history of class struggle, linking this anew to the views of bourgeois historians. In France, the bourgeoisie had won its revolutionary battle against the old superstructure by fighting not only on the political, but on all fronts: on natural science, on philosophy, on economics, and by affirming the need to submit all aspects of social life to examination by Reason.

When it reaches its objective, however, the bourgeoisie becomes conservative. In order to consolidate its power, it reconciles with all who preach peace in society, beginning with religion, and it organises its State as an instrument of control over the new enemy: the proletariat. The bourgeoisie describes the society it thus dominates as everlasting, and produces ideologies, i.e. false representations of reality, to confirm this vision.

As a science, Marxism fights this false consciousness on the theoretical level, but does not confine itself to this: for a century and a half it has pointed the way for those who want to go beyond capitalism, to break through the justifications for exploitation and private accumulation of wealth.

From its inception, the working class is aware of bourgeois oppression, and seeks to react, but: «*early socialism was Utopian socialism. It criticised capitalist society, it condemned and damned it, it dreamed of its destruction, it had visions of a better order, and endeavoured to convince the rich of the immorality of exploitation*».[11]

With Marx and Engels is born scientific socialism, which explains the reasons for capitalist oppression and points the way towards the proletariat's communist revolution.

The bourgeoisie is a class divided by a thousand differences: every capitalist is at war with all the rest, because his success depends on the ruin of the others. In present-day society this permanent conflict is reflected in the clashes between economic groupings, between bands of robber barons who make alliances of convenience with other robber barons, between States and groups of States. Frequently the endemic nature of the conflict becomes armed conflict, exploding at given historical moments into terrifying wars, during which all the productive forces, and all the scientific and technological development which has been achieved, are placed at the service of the destruction of goods, property, and human beings.

Anyone can examine empirically the ways in which our society is profoundly *unjust*, how the promises of *liberty* and *equality* for all, formulated by the bourgeoisie in its revolutionary phase, have not been kept, and how current social relations hamper possibilities of further progress for the human species.

Marxism, however, provides a scientific explanation of society as it now is – its contradictions, its crises, its wars – and does so in order to fight it.

Because of this: « *throughout the civilised world the teachings of Marx evoke the utmost hostility and hatred of all bourgeois science* (because in reality) *in one way or another all official and liberal science defends wage slavery, whereas Marxism has declared relentless war on that slavery* ».[12] This *utmost hostility* has produced a series of distortions of Marxism, which depict it as a crude materialism incapable of seeing anything other than the *economic dimension*, and which would determine all other social relations in a mechanistic fashion.

In fact, to hold that the economy *in the final analysis* determines the superstructure is not to ignore the dialectical relationship that unites the two and that causes them to reciprocally influence each other: the making of laws to regulate international commerce, or the fixing of duties on imports, are examples of the superstructure intervening in the structure. Conversely, we need only think of the studies Marx and Engels dedicated to the theory of the State and its role as an organ of control for the class in power.

But beyond any misunderstanding or misinterpretation, Marxism is a scientific method for analysing reality and how to deal with it. It is our view that in order to establish its validity, it should be treated as any other science, comparing its hypothesis with what we can verify from reality.

It is not possible to reproduce social change in a laboratory experiment – this is why the social sciences are the most difficult – but we can confront the forecasts made by Marx and Engels on the basis of their studies with what later took place, and examine whether history subsequently declared them to be correct.

The creation of the world market: the development of the Pacific basin: the division of society into two opposing classes: the inevitability of the crises of capitalism: the discovery of surplus value: the First World War: these are all examples regarding which we will compare scientific hypothesis and historical fact.

Marxism's scientific *prophecies*

A single world market

«*Modern industry has established the world market, for which the discovery of America paved the way. This market has given an immense development to commerce, to navigation, to communication by land. This development has, in its turn, reacted on the extension of industry; and in proportion as industry, commerce, navigation and railways extended, in the same proportion the bourgeoisie developed, increased its capital, and pushed into the background every class handed down from the Middle Ages. (...) The need of a constantly expanding market for its products chases the bourgeoisie over the entire surface of the globe. It must nestle everywhere, settle everywhere, establish connections everywhere. The bourgeoisie has, through its exploitation of the world market, given a cosmopolitan character to consumption and production in every country*».[13]

These words were written in 1847 and published in the *Communist Party Manifesto*. After more than 160 years, the more honest theoreticians of globalisation have to recognise that no forecast of capitalist world market expansion is more accurate than that of Marx.

Today, it is the norm to see *the production and consumption of all countries as a cosmopolitan process*. We are well aware that frequently we cannot tell exactly where the goods we buy originated: that it is normal to phone a call centre because some electrical appliance has broken down and find ourselves speaking to an operative working in *Romania* or *India*: that it is a common thing to work for multinationals. Similarly, no one is surprised to find, in London, China or Africa, the same MacDonald's with the same menu and the same little tables, and in which one might well be served by immigrant workers born in a different continent.

But this reality would have been difficult to imagine in 1847, when industrial development was affecting a minority of the states then in existence, and when a large part of the human race seemed to be still living in the Middle Ages.

« *To the great chagrin of Reactionists, it (the bourgeoisie) has drawn from under the feet of industry the national ground on which it stood. All old-established national industries have been destroyed or are daily being destroyed. They are dislodged by new industries, whose introduction becomes a life or death question for all civilised nations; by industries that no longer work up indigenous raw material, but raw material drawn from the remotest zones; industries whose products are consumed not only at home, but in every quarter of the globe* ».

Undoubtedly, there is a tendency for industry to lose its *national base*. One example will serve for all: the sponsor of the 2008 Olympic Games was *Lenovo*, the « Chinese » information technology giant. Born in 2003, it initiated a merger with IBM, resurrecting a number of then loss-making ventures. Today the group has 19,000 employees, spread over workplaces scattered all over the world: at work only English is spoken, and *Lenovo* is known as « *the wandering managers' company* »: since it has no central headquarters, meetings are held on a rota basis in North Carolina, Paris or Hong Kong. According to experts on international organisations, this very structure so « *lacking a national base* » facilitates the company's exceptional economic dynamic: 161 million dollars' profit in 2007, forecast to double in 2008.

But take note: when the tensions and crises of the world market deepen, every one of these big groups « *without a national base* » requests the intervention of « *its own State* » whether this be European, American or Chinese imperialism.

What goes for the production of goods, goes for their consumption. In the mid 1800s the vast majority of products were consumed near their point of production, but *Marx* grasped that an « *internationalisation of consumption* » had to match the internationalisation of production.

«*In place of the old wants, satisfied by the production of the country, we find new wants, requiring for their satisfaction the products of distant lands and climes. In place of the old local and national seclusion and self-sufficiency, we have intercourse in every direction and universal inter-dependence of nations*».[14]

Today we sit at a table perhaps made in Vietnam for a Swedish multinational, and eat fish from the Pacific along with vegetables from Africa and fruit from Latin America. We need only glance at any supermarket counter – and read the labels detailing the place of origin of the goods for sale – to verify the existence of *intercourse in every direction and universal inter-dependence of nations.*

And this is true not only of material products: «*As in material, so in intellectual production. The intellectual creations of individual nations become common property. National one-sidedness and narrow-mindedness become more and more impossible, and from the numerous national and local literatures, there arises a world literature*».[15]

Many intellectuals today speak of *cultural contamination* and go into raptures about the meeting of diverse cultures. Marx had foreseen that capitalism would make this possible, establishing a colossal worldwide interconnection and unifying, for the first time in history, the whole human race in a single world market.

«*Now we come to America...*»

When Marx wrote the notes that follow, it was 1850. Capitalist development was concentrated in Great Britain, while the United States was still a young country struggling with the Indian Wars and the slave trade. Yet Marx was able to grasp the coming capitalist development that would bring about a shift in the axis of the world economy.

«*Now we come to America. The most important thing which has happened here, still more important than the February revolution, is the discovery of the Californian gold mines. Even now, after scarcely eighteen months, it can be predicted that this discovery will have much greater consequences than the discovery of America itself (...) The Californian gold mines were only discovered eighteen months ago, and the Yankees have already set about building a railway, a great overland road, and a canal from the Gulf of Mexico, steamships are already regularly steaming from New York to Charges, from Panama to San Francisco, Pacific trade is already concentrating in Panama, and the journey around Cape Horn has become obsolete. A coastline which stretches across thirty degrees of latitude, one of the most beautiful and fertile in the world, and hitherto more or less unpopulated, is now being visibly transformed into a rich, civilised land thickly populated by men of all races, from the Yankee to the Chinese, from the Negro to the Indian to the Malay, from the Creole and the Mestizio to the European*».[16]

Although he was writing in a Europe that considered itself – as indeed it was – the hub of the world, Marx was able to discern the extraordinary development of the United States, but above all, he analysed the enormous future consequences: « *Californian gold is pouring in torrents over America and the Asiatic coast of the Pacific, and is drawing the reluctant barbarian peoples into world trade, into the civilised world. For the second time, world trade has found a new direction. What Tyre, Carthage and Alexandria were in antiquity, Genoa and Venice in the Middle Ages, what London and Liverpool have been hitherto – the emporia of world trade – this is what New York and San Francisco will now become*».[17]

Marx's analysis, therefore, saw how that development involved a second *change of direction*, a change able to shift the economic axis from the Atlantic to the Pacific, after the initial change of direction had shifted it from the Mediterranean to the Atlantic in the 16th century: « *The focal point of international traffic – in the Middle Ages, Italy: in modern times, England – is now the southern half of the North American peninsula*».

Effectively, in the space of half a century, the United States of America became the greatest world power. But Marx further forecast that the shift in the economic axis was such as to also involve Asia.

« *Thanks to Californian gold, and to the Yankees' untiring energies, soon both shores of the Pacific Ocean will be populated, opened up to commerce and industrialised, just as the coast from Boston to San Francisco is now. Then the Pacific Ocean will have the role that the Atlantic has now, the role that in the Middle Ages belonged to the Mediterranean – that of the great maritime highway of world trade; and the Atlantic Ocean will be reduced to the role of an inland sea, as the Mediterranean is now* ».[18]

Any economist can today explain that the salient features of our age are the relative decline of the United States and Europe (hence, of the Atlantic basin) and the rise of China, with its very strong relationship to the American economy (the Pacific basin). Only the tools of Marxism were already able, in the middle of the nineteenth century, to grasp the trends that led to the appearance of these phenomena.

Marx's purpose was not, of course, an academic one: it was fundamental for the prospects of the revolutionary struggle to evaluate the possibilities of further capitalist development: « *it cannot be said that Marx and Engels took a narrow view of the world market, and that they limited its potential to the possible expansion of English capitalism. Thus, they did not envisage that an exhaustion of English capitalist - or even European capitalist - potential on the world market could bring about the collapse of capitalism (...) Marx and Engels held that capitalist development embraces the whole world, but they believed that the contradictions of such development would meantime provoke proletarian revolution in Europe (...) The course of history has run along the lines identified by Marx and Engels. The extension of capitalism into the Pacific basin truly has had « consequences greater than the discovery of America itself* ».[19]

Bourgeoisie and proletarians: capitalism's simplification

Marxism maintains that capitalism produces a great progression towards social simplification, which polarises the bourgeoisie and the proletariat: a polarisation between those who own the means of production and those who sell their labour and *own* nothing but their *prole* (from the Greek: offspring) – that is, the ability to reproduce their own class.

« *In the earlier epochs of history, we find almost everywhere a complicated arrangement of society into various orders, a manifold gradation of social rank. In ancient Rome we have patricians, knights, plebeians, slaves: in the Middle Ages, feudal lords, vassals, guild-masters, journeymen, apprentices, serfs (...) The modern bourgeois society that has sprouted from the ruins of feudal society has not done away with class antagonisms (...) it has simplified them. Society as a whole is more and more splitting up into two great hostile camps, into two great classes directly facing each other – the bourgeoisie and the proletariat* ».[20]

When these words were written in the *Manifesto*, the proletariat, in the strict sense of the word, were a narrow minority of the world population, only a few tens of millions.

How many wage earners are there in the world today? « *"One billion wage-earners for the new century" was our newspaper's headline in 1995, estimating that our class would reach 950 million on a world scale. Today, over a decade later, we can declare this target more than achieved. Current assessments based on* ILO *(International Labour Organisation) statistics, bring this figure to one and a half billion* ».[21]

The division into two large, diametrically opposed classes has been going on without interruption over the last fifty years, and has now spread to every corner of the planet. No one argues that within the two classes there exist complex stratifications - income, lifestyle and cultural differences - but it cannot be denied that the degree of polarisation is enormous. Certainly, it is possible that elements of the proletariat, for reasons of income levels and expectations, do not feel that they belong to this class, but their condition as wage-earners immediately imposes itself on them as soon as events cause the capitalist to stop buying their labour.

Just one example: as early as September 2008, the American Department of Employment advised that for the eighth consecutive month the employment situation was negative, bringing to 605,000 the jobs lost due to the economic situation - workers who have discovered, to their cost, that they belong to a class *diametrically different* from the bosses of Citigroup, Lehman Brothers or Morgan Stanley.

According to Marx, the *simplification* produced by capitalism runs through the whole of society: « *The bourgeoisie, wherever it has got the upper hand, has put an end to all feudal, patriarchal, idyllic relations. It has pitilessly torn asunder the motley feudal ties that bound man to his "natural superiors", and has left remaining no other nexus between man and man than naked self-interest, than callous "cash payment" (...) In one word, for exploitation veiled by religious and political illusions, it has substituted naked, shameless, direct, brutal exploitation (...) it has converted the physician, the lawyer, the priest, the poet, the man of science, into its paid wage labourers. The bourgeoisie has torn away from the family its sentimental veil, and has reduced the family relation to a mere money relation* ».[22]

The society we have before us today is undeniably the society Marx described: a society in which money is the measure of an individual's value, in which everything can be bought and sold, in which those with ideals are seen as at best naive dreamers.

Like Marx, we believe that only *naive dreamers* would think that such a society can last forever.

The discovery of surplus value

« *(The bourgeoisie) has been the first to show what man's activity can bring about. It has accomplished wonders far surpassing Egyptian pyramids, Roman aqueducts, and Gothic cathedrals* » wrote Marx and Engels in the *Manifesto*, acknowledging the largely revolutionary role that the bourgeoisie has played in history.

Marxism maintains that the capitalist system is however tormented by recurrent crises, which in certain cases lead to frightful catastrophes and terrible wars. Marx explains how capitalism itself creates the limits to its own development: « *the true limit of capitalist production is capital itself: it is this: that capital and its appreciation appear as both the point of departure and the point of arrival, as both motivation and goal of production: that production is only production for capital (...) The means – the unconditional development of the forces of production – comes permanently into conflict with the limited end: the appreciation of existing capital* ».[23]

Before Marx, various theories of *appreciation* had been formulated. According to the Physiocratic School, only agriculture was capable of producing riches, while industry limited itself to transforming, and commerce to distributing. With Smith and Ricardo, the idea took hold that value was brought about by labour, and that labour was rewarded by a wage equal to the cost of the essentials for the survival of the worker and his family.

Lenin wrote: « *Classical political economy, before Marx, evolved in England, the most developed of the capitalist countries. Adam Smith and David Ricardo, by their investigations of the economic system, laid the foundations of the labour theory of value. Marx (...) showed that the value of every commodity is determined by the quantity of socially necessary labour time spent on its production. Where the bourgeois economists saw a relation between things (the exchange of one commodity for another) Marx revealed a relation between people. The exchange of commodities expresses the connections between individual producers through the market. Money signifies that the connection is becoming closer and closer, inseparably uniting the entire economic life of the individual producers into one whole.* Capital *signifies a further development of this connection: Man's labour-power becomes a commodity* ».[24]

In the current economic system, the capitalist *invests* money in order to make a profit. He acquires various kinds of commodities: raw materials, labour, and whatever else is required for the process of production: and when the product is made, sells it on the market and obtains a sum of money greater than that invested. This process, familiar and taken for granted in today's society, poses a question: where does it come from, this *surplus* with which the capitalist finds himself at the end of the process, this *surplus value* which originates from the circulation of capital? Marx solves the enigma, demonstrating that it is precisely this commodity – human labour, the labour force – that creates value.

« *The wage-worker sells his labour-power to the owner of land, factories and instruments of labour. The worker spends one part of the day covering the cost of maintaining himself and his family (wages), while the other part of the day he works without remuneration, creating for the capitalist* surplus-value, *the source of profit, the source of the wealth of the capitalist class. The doctrine of surplus-value is the corner-stone of Marx's economic theory* ».[25]

Common sense would hold that to be exploited is to be miserably poor: in fact, the concept of exploitation is a scientific concept, which takes as its starting-point the capitalist's act of expropriation. For example, a European nuclear scientist is *more* exploited than an African farm labourer, because there is a greater difference between what the scientist produces for the capitalist and the remuneration he receives as payment for his labour.

The more capitalism develops, the more small independent producers are transformed into wage labourers. The huge and continuing increase in the numbers of wage labourers on a world scale is due to Marx's discovery: that wage labour creates wealth and valorises capital. Capital wanders through the world seeking its reservoirs of surplus value – new wage labourers to exploit.

Today the imperialist bourgeoisie no longer requires to debate a theory of surplus value: they own the surplus value, and are cutting each other's throats for a share of the spoils. The proletariat, the producers of surplus value, have been defeated, and are not strong enough to force a debate on the true nature of surplus value, because such a debate would be a debate about the subversion of bourgeois society, and therefore about the nature and necessity of proletarian revolution.

The imperialist bourgeoisie knows that the proletariat are the producers of surplus value: this is evident from their agonising need either to achieve absolute surplus value, by moving factories to Asia and Africa, where labour is cheaper and by working immigrants and children in sub-human conditions; or to increase relative surplus value, by developing science and technology and reducing the labour force in high-technology industries.

The bourgeoisie's thirst for surplus value can been seen in the struggle without quarter between the various fractions within every State. Moreover, what else are the attempts to « *reform the State* » if not attempts to reduce the share of surplus value expended on economic parasitism, in order to increase the share of those bourgeois fractions engaged in competition for world markets.

In its spasmodic attempts to assure itself ever-increasing quantities of surplus value, the bourgeoisie ends up by incessantly increasing the size of its rival class, of those who – as Marx writes in the *Manifesto – have nothing to lose* (from a revolution) *but their chains. And have a world to gain.*

A world war of a violence never before seen

We have said that to understand reality is to be prepared for the way in which events follow on one another, and hence to be able to act, by intervening in history. To be able to do this, Marxism must get down to the basis on which the confrontation between the powers takes place, analysing rise and decline, and studying the consequences of this dynamic: «*After giving it first place in his revolutionary activity, Marx also recommended to the First International the study of "the mysteries of international politics". Already, in the* Manifesto *of 1848, with the creation of the capitalist world market, the world was seen as "a universal dependence of one nation on another". Today this dependence has become so stringent that it requires a global analysis of each substantive act in international politics, and above all, of the conditions that have paved the way for it*».[26]

In 1887 there had never been a world war. Until then, wars had only marginally involved the civilian population, and almost exclusively the civilian population of those areas of a country in which a war was being fought: to give some idea of numbers, in the famous battle of Waterloo there were 50,000 casualties, all soldiers. The general atmosphere was one of great optimism about economic development, while in philosophy Positivism, with its unshakeable faith in science, looked forward to a future of uninterrupted progress.

But Engels could see that this economic development was incubating storms of dimensions never previously known, and that the emergence of new powers would unleash a conflict such as the human race had never experienced: «*And, finally, the only war left for Prussia-Germany to wage will be a world war, a world war, moreover, of an extent and violence hitherto unimagined. Eight to a million soldiers will be at each other's throats, and in the process they will strip Europe barer than a swarm of locusts. The depredations of the Thirty Years' War compressed into three to four years and extended over the entire continent: famine, disease, the universal lapse into barbarism, both of the armies and of the people, in the wake of acute misery: irretrievable dislocation of our artificial system of trade, industry and credit, ending in universal bankruptcy: collapse of the old states and their conventional political wisdom to the point where crowns will roll into the gutters by the dozen, and no one will be around to pick them up: the absolute impossibility of foreseeing how it will all end and who will emerge as victor from the battle. Only one consequence is absolutely certain: universal exhaustion and the creation of the conditions for the ultimate victory of the working class. That is the prospect for the moment when the systematic development of mutual one-upman-ship in armaments reaches its climax and finally brings forth its inevitable fruits. This is the pass, my worthy princes and statesmen, to which you in your wisdoms have brought our ancient Europe*».[27]

Twenty-eight years later, for the first time in history, an immense body of soldiers fought, over a period of *three or four years,* a war which saw 10 million dead, while *hunger, epidemics and general savagery* caused over 6 million civilian victims. Many were *the crowns that rolled into the gutters:* to cite only the most important, the Austro-Hungarian Empire and the Ottoman Empire fell apart, in Russia the Tsar fell, and the German Empire went into crisis.

Lenin was to complete the study of the new strategic phase, but in *Anti-Duhring* Engels had gathered various aspects of the future development of society: « *he picks out the incipient transformation of capitalist enterprises into joint stock companies, and the trend of development towards "collective capitalism", State capitalism. Engels directs a powerful beam of theoretical light on the turn of century crisis, and brilliantly anticipates another new and unheard-of phenomenon: capitalism's worldwide war* ».[28]

On yet another level, Engels' prediction came true: the war created the *necessary conditions for the final victory of the working class.* It created the *objective conditions*, and where there existed the *subjective intervention* of a revolutionary party, as in Russia, the war opened up the road to proletarian revolution.

The accuracy of Engels' predictions induced Lenin to write, on 29th June 1918: « *Nobody, thank God, believes in miracles nowadays. Miraculous prophecy is a fairy-tale. But scientific prophecy is a fact. And in these days, when we so very often encounter shameful despondency and even despair around us, it is useful to recall one scientific prophecy which has come true (...) What genius is displayed in this prophecy! And how infinitely rich in ideas is every sentence of this exact, clear, brief and scientific class analysis*! ».[29]

So, no miraculous prophecies, but concrete verifications of a scientific method for interpreting reality. This is why Marxism is today still able to provide answers and pointers for the future: it provided them for those who, like Lenin, were able – if only briefly – to defeat the domination of the bourgeoisie: it will provide them for the young revolutionaries who tomorrow will take up the interrupted journey. But the *possibility* of revolution is indissolubly bound up with science: it is the consciousness of what *must be done* that shows the way, that can provide the right tool – the revolutionary party: that can indicate the fault lines along which the balance between the powers will crack, and thus the historic moment in which there will be a concrete opening to the possibility of social revolution. Marxist science is what makes the difference between a rebellion and a victorious revolution.

Chapter 2

The Age of Imperialism

« We are undoubtedly living at the juncture of two epochs, and the historic events that are unfolding before our eyes can be understood only if we analyse, in the first place, the objective conditions of the transition from one epoch to the other (...) We have important historical epochs: in each of them there are and will always be individual and partial movements, now forward, now backward; there are and will always be various deviations from the average type and mean tempo of the movement (...) The first epoch, from the Great French Revolution to the Franco-Prussian War, is one of the rise of the bourgeoisie, of its triumph, of the bourgeoisie on the upgrade, an epoch of bourgeois-democratic movements in general, and of bourgeois-national movements in particular: an epoch of the rapid breakdown of the obsolete feudal-absolutist institutions. The second epoch is that of the full domination and decline of the bourgeoisie, one of transition from its progressive character towards reactionary and even ultra-reactionary finance capital. This is an epoch in which a new class – present-day democracy – is preparing and slowly mustering its forces. The third epoch, which has just set in, places the bourgeoisie in the same "position" as that in which the feudal lords found themselves during the first epoch. This is the epoch of imperialism and imperialist upheavals, as well as of upheavals stemming from the nature of imperialism ».

Lenin, *"Under A False Flag"* 1915

Between 1870 and 1913 there took place the process that many academics call *the first globalisation.* It was a period of extraordinary capitalist development, both in terms of the increase in industrial production and in its extension to new parts of the world. In this period, total industrial production increased fivefold, with exceptional peaks in some sectors: for example, steel production grew from 70 thousand to 65 million tons.

New branches of industry – petrol, electrical and chemical (agricultural fertilisers, explosives, food colouring) – were born, while a series of scientific discoveries revolutionised daily life. The internal combustion engine and the diesel engine were invented, with all their implications for the development of greater mobility in overland, maritime and aerial transport: the invention of refrigeration opened up new perspectives for the food industry and for trade; the telegraph, the telephone, the radio and the cinema were born, while new discoveries in the field of medicine gave birth to the pharmaceutical industry and facilitated a reorganisation of health care, permitting people to live longer, and in particular combating infant mortality.

These were changes that, in less than a generation, transformed people's daily lives, creating a climate of optimism and faith in the future, and from this sprang the philosophy of *positivism.* The *common sense* of the age held that *capitalism had changed* and that the harsher aspects of capitalist oppression could eventually be overcome by economic development.

Capitalism spreads into new areas where there are plentiful supplies of raw materials and cheap labour, and this provides an advantage to the older states, which can thereby allow the odd extra crumb to trickle down to their working classes.

Enterprises, however, have a tendency to grow in order to stand up to competition as it moves from a national to a global base, and to form themselves into ever-expanding agglomerations, seeking out a monopoly position within their particular sector.

Finance capital becomes more and more important, since growing economic enterprises seek ever-greater centralisation, and, as predicted by Marx, the whole credit sector, the Exchange and its financial intermediaries, grow alongside.

The British economist John A. Hobson carried out an important analysis of this new phase, being also the first to use the term *Imperialism*, the title of his 1902 book. Even Lenin made use of this work, and completed a colossal analysis of the new phase, compiling 21 jotters full of notes, with extracts from 148 books, and 232 articles that had appeared in 49 different periodicals.

In 1916, he summarised this material in his critical essay, which not coincidentally was entitled « *Imperialism, the supreme phase of capitalism* ». Lenin breaks with the ruling ideology, which sees capitalism as « a form of politics » – e.g. the politics of finance capital thwarted by industrial capital – and specifies that imperialism is the universal political form of the mature bourgeois mode of production.

Lenin writes: *« (...) we must give a definition of imperialism that will include the following five of its basic features:*

the concentration of production and capital has developed to such a high stage that it has created monopolies which play a decisive role in economic life;

the merging of bank capital with industrial capital and the creation, on the basis of this "financial capital" of a financial oligarchy;

the export of capital as distinguished from the export of commodities acquires exceptional importance;

the formation of international monopolist capitalist associations which share out the world amongst themselves;

the territorial division of the whole world among the biggest capitalist powers is completed.

Imperialism is capitalism at that stage of development at which the dominance of monopolies and finance capital is established; in which the export of capital has acquired pronounced importance; in which the division of the world among international trusts has begun, in which the division of all territories of the globe among the biggest capitalist powers has been completed».[30]

History has demonstrated that Lenin hit the nail on the head. The world that confronts us today is the world his book described: the presence of big multinationals, the great significance of finance capital, the growing importance of international movement of capital, the clashes for a share of the world market, and the way the big powers divide the world into spheres of influence.

Lenin also hit on another important aspect of the wage stratification present in those States that had reached imperialist maturity: that excess profit serves to *corrupt* the upper strata of the proletariat, guaranteeing their support for imperialist policies and binding them to the imperialism of their respective countries.

The political phenomenon of reformism, originating from the meddling of the petit bourgeoisie in the lives of the proletariat, is thus transformed into «*opportunism*» and «*social chauvinism*».

When capitalism's uneven development, and the emergence of new powers – the USA and Germany were the China and India of their day – marked the end of the *first globalisation*, the bourgeoisie of the different nations called the proletariat to arms in defence of bourgeois interests and for a fresh division of the spheres of influence. Lenin made clear the inevitability of war: «*The only conceivable basis under capitalism for the division of spheres of influence, interests, colonies, etc, is a calculation of the strength of those participating, their general economic, financial, military strength, etc. And the strength of these participants in the division does not change to an equal degree, for the even development of different undertakings, trusts, branches of industry or countries is impossible under capitalism*».[31]

Uneven development causes imbalances in relations between powers: when these imbalances surpass a certain level, the inevitable instrument of correction is war: « *Half a century ago Germany was a miserable, insignificant country, if her capitalist strength is compared with that of the Britain of that time; Japan compared with Russia in the same way. Is it "conceivable" that in ten or twenty years' time the relative strength of the imperialist powers will have remained unchanged? It is out of the question* ».[32]

As forecast, the opportunists gave mass assent to the imperialist war, swinging between open interventionism and impotent pacifism. Only those who had been vaccinated by *proletarian internationalism* were able to hold firm, and knew what action to take in the terrifying explosion of violence that was the *Great War*, the first imperialist war.

That conflict opened a new phase, in which it became obvious that the more capitalism developed, the greater were its contradictions, its wars and its violence: but the proletariat could look to another possibility – that when the *break-down of order* unleashed war, it could also trigger the process of revolutionary crisis. But this required a *subjective* factor: the existence of a political party with a clear strategic vision, a party aware that the proletariat had the capacity to become « a power among the powers ».

A party independent in terms of theory, organisation and finance: that for years previously had been able to root itself in the working class and become a respected and valued point of reference: that had been able to speak to the young, selecting groups of militants ready to place revolutionary activity above all else.

Lenin's strategic elaboration, united with the organisational model from *What is to be done?* allowed the Russian sector of the international proletariat to transform imperialist war into social revolution, and to become the model for the international proletariat of the present and of the future.

The breaking of the weak link in the chain, Russia, did not lead to the breaking of the strong link, Germany. The revolutionary process was interrupted: the reaction of the ruling class, the international imperialist bourgeoisie, was a terrible one, assuming different forms according to the history, economy and politics of the various powers – a difference that can be roughly summarised in the forms of democracy and of fascism.

In Russia, as Lenin had foreseen, reaction took on nationalist characteristics, in the shape of Stalinism. Its first objective was to strike at the Bolshevik Party's internationalist strategy. Reaction transformed itself into a bureaucratic apparatus at the service of the Russian bourgeoisie, from the big state-capitalist groups to the small farmers, with both bureaucracy and State party protecting and guaranteeing the national interest.

Leon Trotsky said that in the process of deforming the Russian party, *the true Bolsheviks disappeared like flies in milk*: in fact, the nationalist overthrow of all the Bolshevik policies required a work of extermination of the avant-garde who had remained faithful to the ideals of internationalism. The final and most famous act was the assassination of Trotsky himself, then in exile in Mexico, in 1940.

For years intellectuals have argued that there is a *continuity* between Leninism and Stalinism. Lenin maintained that socialist revolution was by its nature international revolution, and that the Russian proletarian State had to place itself at the service of international revolution, a position coherent with the strategy he had formulated: Stalinism defended the ideology of *socialism in one country*, which was coherent with the nationalist strategy of the Russian State, and which held that the first duty of all the Communist parties in the world was the defence of Russia: it is extremely difficult to find elements of continuity between these two positions.

The counter-revolution struck hard at the working-class movement, which found itself so completely disarmed that – proof that lack of a theoretical base always carries a high price – at the outbreak of the Second World War there were no attempts at revolution.

Once again, the validity of the Leninist lesson was confirmed: the massacres and the devastation of the First

World War paled before the violence of the Second, yet in spite of the fact that significant sectors of the proletariat took part in armed movements such as the European Resistance, there was no attempt to overthrow the domination of the bourgeoisie.

«*It is true that objectively the proletariat moves according to the contradictions of capitalism. But it is simplistic to hold that a crisis "inevitably triggers the revolutionary will of the proletariat". Besides, the appalling massacre of the Second World War, unlike the First a waste of time and energy for revolutionary strategy, and a gift on a plate to the bourgeoisie, demonstrates the contrary*».[33]

The powerless position of the proletariat did not change in the post-war period. After Yalta, the world seemed to be divided in two, between the defenders of «*freedom and democracy*» and the supporters of the «*socialist*» camp, a division that cut across Europe, enlisting everyone on one side or the other.

In Italy, however, some young people who had taken part in the *Resistance* began to ask questions: Why had internationalism been unable to find a voice, as had happened in the previous world conflict? What was the true nature of the USSR? Was Lenin's analysis of imperialism still valid? What could be done to pick up the threads of an autonomous working-class opposition?

Starting from an anti-Stalinist position, these young people soon realised that the reason for the powerlessness of the working class arose from its having abandoned or incompletely assimilated the experiences of Leninism: there then began the difficult work of reclaiming the tools of Marxist analysis and the re-establishment of a Leninist current of thought. The founding group of Lotta Comunista formulated the *Theses of 1957*.

«*Focusing squarely on the "development of imperialism" on the unity of the world market, on the variety of powers within the ambit of the "advanced industrialised countries", and on the emergence of new powers in Asia, the "Theses of 1957" established in its final form the scientific synthesis of "unitary imperialism"*».[34] The world market was all a unit, as was imperialism: the USSR was an imperialist country, with State capitalism as its central feature: no true division had taken place at Yalta, rather a concession to the USSR by Europe, in order to delay – in the interests of the USA – the rebirth of Germany as a major power and to impede any tendency towards its unification, although this was to be the prime objective of a wider European unification.

Lenin's analysis of imperialism, however, was still valid. The balance between the powers was an unstable one: capitalism's uneven development would continue to give rise to changes that would take time to come to a head before suddenly bursting forth. There was to be the European renaissance, Japan's recovery, and in Asia – epicentre of imperialist tensions – capitalist development would lead to the emergence of new major powers such as India and China.

In 1968 Arrigo Cervetto wrote: « *There was no division of the world at Yalta, because the United States, having conquered it, did not have to divide it with anyone, still less with the USSR, which came out of the war on its knees. The USA ceded Eastern Europe and the Balkans to the USSR. The USA ceded not its own markets, but those of European imperialism, and kept for itself all the rest. As the saying goes, the USA killed two birds with one stone, except that both the birds and the stone belonged to someone else: and tied Russia for an indefinite period to a coalition that was a liability and to markets that the USSR could only exploit and maintain by military force and by preventing them from falling under the influence of resurgent German imperialism. The USSR would certainly be the stronger for taking over the Eastern European markets, but would have to defend them from German penetration – as it has been doing now for more than ten years. And Russian strength, if not overwhelming, as evidenced by the growing invasion of its markets by the European Common Market, would slow down the development of German power, and consequently the development of the other European powers* ».

The real winner of the Second World War was the USA – no coincidence that in 1945 it was responsible for almost half of world industrial production – while: « *Great Britain and the Soviet Union, although it was also in their interests that Germany and Japan should come out of the conflict defeated and cut down to size (...) ended up paying a high price, at least in the post-war decade, for the final solution that ended the war: a solution agreed with the* USA, *but above all willed and imposed by American power».*[35]

When this point of view was voiced, in the immediate post-war period, it seemed as far removed as could be imagined from common sense, but it was accurate. From the very beginning, it was obvious that the USSR was having difficulty in holding onto the immense sphere of influence assigned to it, and that it was being forced to impose its imperialist control by force of arms, while Europe, albeit divided and weakened, was experiencing a period of intense development – the so-called *Thirty Glorious Years* – which, within the space of a generation, brought it to substantial economic and technological recovery in relation to the United States.

Moreover, the definitive winding-up of colonial empires all over the world supplied capitalist production with immense new *reservoirs of surplus value.*

After the end of the Second World War, capitalism throughout the world took an extraordinary leap forward. In 1993, Arrigo Cervetto drew attention to the sub-editor of *The Economist*, Clive Cook, who held that the spread of the market economy in the so-called Third World was much more significant than the fall of the USSR and its empire.

« *The London weekly glories in the "triumph of capitalism" in its "various types" – American, European, Japanese. For we Marxists, this is a case of a natural historic world process, of the spread of capitalism throughout the world, of the law of movement discovered by Marx, the validity of which we have always believed (...) True, for a good part of human history, the rate of economic change has been close to zero. It is also true that the current world rate of 2 % per year means that in 35 years, world production has doubled. We have no problem acknowledging a triumph of capitalism, precisely because it is a triumph of uneven development, and an accelerated growth of the economic and political contradictions of this mode of production, its class struggles, its wars and its revolutions».*[36]

In the post-war period, *uneven development* immediately displayed itself in the rapid recovery of Japan, Germany and Italy, while the independence acquired by the former colonies – e.g. India – opened the way to their growth.

This previously unknown cycle of development was not a peaceful one, although the end of the Second World War saw a resumption of the hypocritical chorus « *never again war* » and saw the UN, which took the place of the old failed *League of Nations,* emphatically proclaim the intention of its members to « *save future generations from the scourge of war* ».

It is absurd even to give the name « *peace* » to the period that followed the end of the Second World War: « *according to the International Institute for Strategic Studies (IISS) of London, between 1945 and 2000 there have been 188 cases of armed conflict, covering the whole world and involving 90 countries, with the high toll of 22,456,000 victims* ».[37]

The long list of the countries over which imperialism has fought its period of peace stretches from *Afghanistan* to *Zimbabwe*. These are wars fought by all and every means, from napalm in Vietnam to gas in the Iran-Iraq war, from the machetes of the clashes between Hutu and Tutsi in Rwanda to the « ethnic cleansing » of the wars of European unification in the former Yugoslavia. One thing these wars have in common is the systematic involvement of the civilian population, an unmistakable feature of imperialist war.

Imperialism has not changed, and within its future growth smoulder new and more terrible conflicts. To look at the history of the twentieth century helps us to understand what we can do to confront them, in order not to become impotent and submissive victims: what stands out from the events of this tormented century is the superiority of Leninism in relation to other currents of the working-class movement.

We are Leninists because with his analysis Lenin understood the society of his day and its contradictions: we are Leninists because it was with Lenin that the proletariat, in the terrible storm of the First World War, pointed the way to the emancipation of our class. And we are Leninists because twenty years later, in a more widespread war, with a more numerous working class and with deeper dissensions within imperialism itself, the proletariat, lacking its own strategic party, continued to be controlled by its respective imperialist powers.

Examining the history of the *century of imperialism* will help us to be prepared when a fresh *breakdown of order* opens a new chapter of this age of crises, wars and revolutions.

An age of crises, wars and revolutions

The killing industry

« *We are as are in autumn / the leaves on the trees* »: so Giuseppe Ungaretti, a youthful veteran who was subsequently to become one of the greatest Italian poets of the twentieth century, in July 1918 described the mood of the soldiers in the trenches of the First World War. Like many other young intellectuals of his time, and despite his anarchist and socialist sympathies, he too had failed to understand that the coming war would be very different from the nineteenth-century rebellions that had supported national independence, and having volunteered for the front, was to experience its full horror.

Paul Frölich estimates that 10 million fell in battle, and that 5 million civilians were killed in the course of the Great War.[38] Soldiers were drawn up and ordered into mass attacks according to traditional tactics, but the use of the machine-gun – first tried out during the American Civil War – and of modern artillery, aircraft, gas and the first tanks, caused horrendous slaughter.

Imperialism had developed a new and flowering industry: the killing industry.

In the whole of the Battle of the Marne, which opened the conflict on the Western Front, 3.5 million troops were committed on two fronts, with a toll of 400 thousand dead and one million wounded: at Verdun, the most recent estimate from historians is 420 thousand dead and around 800 thousand suffering from gas-poisoning or wounded.

Mario Silvestri, in *The decline of Western Europe*, estimates a loss of 6 % of the population of Western Europe as a result of the war, and reports the results of a study of the

German male population, which documents that over half of young German males between the ages of 20 and 24 died or were wounded in the war.

« *The outbreak of the First World War transformed the light-hearted rhythms of the Roaring Twenties into the roar of bombs. As Erich Maria Remarque said, "a generation, even if it escaped the grenades, was destroyed by the war..." Remarque was right. The destruction was not just physical* ».[39]

Frölich describes the effects of the conflict on Europe: « *the war machine has passed through this entire continent from one end to the other, and over a long period. The war has razed villages and cities to the ground, it has transformed whole provinces into piles of rubble, it has devastated the harvests of great countries and destroyed a huge number of factories. A swathe of territory thousands of miles long and some miles wide has been completely wiped out: roads and bridges have disappeared, enormous forests hacked down. From the earth great treasures have been ripped: coal, metals and other raw materials that have ended up as dust, destroying even as they were themselves destroyed. A huge number of trains have been lost, and a gigantic fleet sunk. Herds of millions of animals have disappeared. A whole culture has been annihilated. Only one step forward has been achieved: the human spirit has worked miracles with the technology of destruction* ».[40]

It was in consideration of the horrors of the war that on 28th June 1919, the Treaty of Versailles provided for the setting up of the *League of Nations*, with the aim of « *controlling international armaments, promoting well being and quality of life on Earth, and preventing war and encouraging diplomacy as a means of managing conflict between States* ».

But the re-establishment of imperialist order in 1918 was not sufficient to guarantee a new balance. In 1929 came the terrible economic crisis, which via the thousand interwoven threads of international finance struck the whole world, causing industrial production in the real economy to collapse. And when the chickens of 1918 and 1929 came home to roost, no *League of Nations* could avert the new catastrophe.

Pacifists hold that war is an *error*, or arises from the personality of whichever warmonger is currently in power:

communists know that war « *is no chance happening, no "sin", as is thought by Christian priests (who are no whit behind the opportunists in preaching patriotism and peace) but an inevitable stage of capitalism, just as legitimate a form of the capitalist way of life as peace is* ».[41]

Recalling von Clausewitz, Lenin reminds us that: « *War is simply the continuation of politics by other (i.e violent) means* » and that imperialist war is inevitable because: « *the partition of the world compels the capitalists to go over from peaceful expansion to an armed struggle for the repartitioning of colonies and spheres of influence* ».[42]

War on war

In the course of the First World War, the ruling class had to face the spontaneous refusal of the war that manifested itself in all the armies involved: a refusal it met with decimations, tribunals and the exhortations of the churches. Only the conscious intervention of internationalists could have transformed that *yearning for peace* into a *conscious war* against bourgeois society.

To the national solidarity between classes urged by the bourgeoisie, the Bolsheviks opposed international solidarity between the oppressed, and took up anew the watchword « *the enemy is in our own house* » to interpret the instinctive rejection of the war which could be clearly observed among the proletariat at the Front.

« *The British "Labour" Leader of January 7 1915 published a series of quotations from the British bourgeois Press on instances of fraternisation between British and German soldiers, who arranged a "forty-eight hour truce" at Christmas, met amicably in no-man's land, and so on. The British military authorities issued a special order forbidding fraternisation* » wrote Lenin in March 1915. « *Try to imagine (*the socialist leaders*), instead of aiding the bourgeoisie, something they are now engaged in, forming an international committee to agitate for "fraternisation* *and attempts to establish friendly relations" between the socialists of the belligerent countries, both in the "trenches" and among the troops in general. What would the results be several months from now*».[43]

In 1917 alone, there was mutiny in the German and English navies, a revolt in the French army, and a workers' uprising in Turin. At last the revolutionary situation presented itself, and the Bolsheviks were ready to make use of it.

«*To the Marxist it is indisputable that a revolution is impossible without a revolutionary situation: furthermore, it is not every revolutionary situation that leads to revolution. What, generally speaking, are the symptoms of a revolutionary situation? We shall certainly not be mistaken if we indicate the following three major symptoms: (1) when it is impossible for the ruling classes to maintain their rule without any change: when there is a crisis, in one form or another, among the "upper classes", a crisis in the policy of the ruling class, leading to a fissure through which the discontent and indignation of the oppressed classes bursts forth. For a revolution to take place, it is usually insufficient for "the lower classes not to want" to live in the old way; it is also necessary that "the upper classes should be unable" to live in he old way; (2) when the suffering and want of the oppressed classes have grown more acute than usual; (3) when, as a consequence of the above causes, there is a considerable increase in the activity of the masses, who uncomplainingly allow themselves to be robbed in "peace time", but in turbulent times, are drawn both by all the circumstances of the crisis, and by the "upper classes" themselves into independent historical action. Without these objective changes, which are independent of the will, not only of individual groups and parties, but even of individual classes, a revolution, as a general rule, is impossible. The totality of all these objective changes is called a revolutionary situation*».[44]

But a revolutionary situation on its own is not enough. The objective situation needs to be matched by a subjective intervention: «*it is not every revolutionary situation that gives rise to a revolution; revolution arises only out of a situation in which the above-mentioned objective changes are accompanied by a subjective change, namely, the ability of the revolutionary class to take revolutionary mass action strong enough to break (or dislocate) the old government, which never, not even in a period of crisis, "falls" if it is not toppled over*».[45]

On 10th October, the Bolshevik Central Committee decided on an uprising. The *Revolutionary Military Committee* led by *Trotsky* began to organise the Red Army: when the government tried to arrest its members and outlaw the Bolshevik Press, the uprising began.

On 24th October St. Petersburg was occupied, members of the government arrested, and the Winter Palace and the barracks of counter-revolutionary army detachments attacked. There were no casualties at this early stage, the well-prepared nature of the uprising allowing losses to be limited. By the morning of 25th October, the new government could already make its first proclamation: « *The cause for which the people have fought – the immediate offer of a democratic peace, the abolition of the great landed properties, the workers' control of production, the creation of government by the soviets – this cause has been secured*».

The Bolsheviks kept their promises: the first action of the revolution was the declaration of peace, providing for the immediate and unilateral suspension of hostilities and the abolition of secret diplomacy, and the secret treaties Russia had made with the other imperialist countries were openly denounced.

It was such a clear line that even Henry Kissinger, in his book *The Art Of Diplomacy* acknowledges that the objectives of the Bolsheviks differed from those of the whole of international diplomacy.

« *Nothing remotely like the Soviet Union had appeared on the horizon of European diplomacy since the time of the French Revolution. For the first time in more than a century, a country had officially dedicated itself to overturning the established order, even proposing to abolish the State: after which, as Lenin said, there would be no need for either diplomacy or foreign policy (...) none of the early Communist leaders thought that a socialist state could co-exist for decades with capitalist countries (...) the main objective was to promote world revolution, not to manage relations between states*».

After the terrible massacres of the Spanish Civil War – the testing-ground for new techniques of extermination, such as carpet bombing of the civilian population – in 1939 the human race was again flung into a conflict beside which the violence of the Great War was but a pale shadow.

A hidden page of history

During the Second World War, the bourgeoisie was ready to repress protest against the war and the society that had produced it. In spite of this, even where counter-revolution took the most brutal forms of repression, in Nazi Germany, there were episodes of working-class resistance and opposition. A little-known page of history, but the movements it records were by no means negligible, especially if one considers that the notorious Nazi lagers were first established in 1933 specifically for the detention of German political opponents: « *On 21st March 1933, a Monaco daily newspaper carries this announcement: "On Wednesday 22nd March the first concentration camp, accommodating five thousand, will be opened on the outskirts of Dachau. We have taken this decision leaving aside all ignoble caution, convinced that we are acting in the interests of national pacification and according to the wishes of the population: Heinricht Himmler" (from "The Torturers Speak" Vincenzo & Luigi Pappalettera, Ed. Mursia 1979). Starting with four thousand arrests of* KPD *(German Communist Party) members carried out immediately after the Reichstag fire, thanks to lists prepared by the Prussian government headed by Goering's predecessors, the social democrats C. Severing and O. Braun, by the end of 1933 forty thousand were sentenced for political offences* ».[46]
The numbers of German opponents of Nazism affected by the repression is striking: J. Nobecourt in *Le Monde* maintains that between 1933 and 1939, one million Germans passed through the concentration camps.
In the front line was the working class, which paid a heavy price: « *It was the working class that brought the most weight and strength to the opposition to Nazism: all writers on this subject agree that the Nazi party experienced the greatest difficulty in getting a foothold in the factories. In 1935, the Nazi leaders had to suspend the elections for representatives to workplace Worker-Management*

Once more new scientific and technical discoveries, and all the ongoing development of productive forces, were employed in killing. Imperialism stops for nothing: not when, in the guise of Nazism, it plans the slave labour of the lagers (the invention of which must be credited to democratic Great Britain during the 1905 Boer War): nor when, in the guise of the *Allied liberators* it employs carpet bombing to exterminate the civilian populations of the

Committees, since their members were failing to win the votes of the workers. This is even more significant if we consider that the German working class had already been subjected to years of Nazi propaganda and repressions against internationalists ».[47]

Internationalists were subjected to the double persecution of Nazism and Stalinism. A study of the KPD documents the extent of the massacres: « *According to Hermann Weber's new investigation of the KPD's history ("German Communists" Ed. Dietz, Berlin 2004) of the 300,000 members of the party in 1932, a total of 150,000 were arrested at least once up to 1945, and 20,000 were killed, of which 2,000 in just the first two years of the regime. Of the approximately 1,400 people who made up the leadership of the KPD, 400 were killed in various circumstances : of these, 222 by the Nazis and 178 by the Stalinists: while of the 59 members who had previously held political office, 6 were killed by the Nazis and 8 by Stalinism* ».[48]

In spite of these levels of repression, the opponents of Nazism continued to work within the German working class for a long time: « *In 1944, the KPD was carrying out illegal activities in Argus and in Teves, in Wittenau: in Hasse & Wrede in Marzahn and in Loewe in Moabit: but also in the bigger and more significant factories such as Siemens and AEG in Wedding. In Teves there were 40 paid-up "supporters" out of 2,000 employees, in Argus 30 out of 2,5000: and all took part in spreading the word, distributing written material and collecting funds for their illegal work. In Siemens there was a group of 20 to 25 comrades, among whom were Rudolf Seiffert and Erich Schulz, both of whom were to lose their lives (...) by the end of 1944 there were hundreds of arrests, and 90 dead or executed, among them Saefkow, Jacob and Bastlein* ».[49]

Although lacking a strategy, the German working class opposed the counter-revolution with everything at their disposal – their will and their organisational capacity – often paying a tragic price.

European mainland: not even when *the biggest democracy in the world* tries out the new atomic weapon on Hiroshima and Nagasaki, annihilating 200,000 civilians.

The Second World War reproduces the horrors of the First « *on a bigger scale. K. Marx's "Capital" was published in 1867. Since then, world capital has multiplied twenty fold (...) Fifty years later, when Lenin raised the banner of proletarian revolution again, world capital had tripled. The increase in capital's power became an increase in its destructive ability, which unleashed, for the first time in history, a World War. Twenty years went by and the World War was repeated. The world's value-producing capital was double what had brought about the first global conflict. Double capital, double war. When the conflict ended, world capital was six times what it had been when Marx's "Capital" saw the light. Over the past forty years without a world war, world capital has tripled. This means that it is three times more destructive than it was at the end of the Second World War, in spite of the destruction it suffered* ».[50]

In the Second World War, *double capital* meant *double war,* which also raged on the Asian shores of the Pacific, by then involved in the growth of imperialism: « *overall, the combatant dead of the Second World War numbered 15 million, on a demographic base that was wider and over a longer period of time than had been the case during the First, in which the fallen were 10 million (...) The fate of the civilian populations was quite different. Compared with some tens of thousand dead from direct warfare in the First World War, in the Second the civilian dead were at least 40 million* ».[51]

In effect, the killing industry had become more efficient and had increased its turnover. « *From the many testimonies, memoirs and autobiographies of the winners and the losers, what emerges is how a modern war is also, if not mainly, an enormous organisational issue. In the Blitzkrieg which brought France to its knees, the crucial penetration of the Ardennes required the concentration, on a front of 115 kilometres, of an armed mass which, if drawn up along a single road, would have had its head in Treviri, on the Rhine, and its tail in Königsberg, in eastern Prussia (...) An impressive organisational problem was the operation by which the British, taking advantage of a pause in hostilities conced-*

ed by a Hitler still seeking a compromise, evacuated 338 thousand troops from Dunkirk in less than ten days: and conversely, the famous Normandy Landings, which co-ordinated a variety of 6 thousand sea transports with more than 350 warships of different calibres, a thousand minesweepers, and more than 6 thousand aircraft – bombers, reconnaissance, passenger planes and amphibians».[52]

The pride of imperialism is appalling: « *Of its kind, the air attack which in the single night of 9th March 1945 unloaded on Tokyo 1,600 tons of incendiaries, killing or maiming 185 thousand people and razing to the ground 39 kilometres square of the city, was a brilliant example of organisational capacity. The accounts of those who orchestrated such operations, and of the many others like it that characterised the Second World War, betray pride for the problems solved and for a job well done, while the ensuing consequences seem, incredibly, to fade into the background. It seems irrelevant that the measure of that organisational capacity was how well it destroyed and how many it massacred*».[53]

If in only twenty years we have progressed from the trenches of the Karst (*Alpine region which at the time of WW1 was part of the Italo-Austrian frontier, and a theatre of war*) to Hiroshima, how much violence will the *killing industry* be capable of summoning up tomorrow, after decades of more capitalist development?

Yalta, the nadir of internationalism

The Yalta Conference held between 4th and 11th February 1945, in which Franklin Delano Roosevelt, Winston Churchill and Stalin took part, came to be seen as the get-together during which the victors of the Second World War divided up the world into spheres of influence. The split that ran across Germany, and across Berlin itself, was in effect to last up to 1989, and provided for the whole of eastern Europe to be dominated by Russian imperialism.

The charlatans of false socialism

During the 1960s, when the cycle of state capitalism was in its final stages, socialism continued to grow by order.
New socialist states sprang up from one day to the next, and were enthusiastically christened by the « in-house intellectuals » of the left-wing parties of the western metropolises. Years have now gone by, and we have had first-hand experience of history's endless fantasies.
Moscow was the Mecca of socialism achieved, then Peking followed its perfect example. Tito's Belgrade, with all its oddities, was socialist, and so was Oxa's Albania, albeit with its own peculiar habit of looking to Peking: Bulgaria and Cuba were socialist, and there were socialist states in Africa and in the whole of the Third World. If a state entered Moscow's sphere of influence, it became socialist as if by magic: and so part of the human race found itself living in an enchanted hothouse in which social emancipation had reached its peak. Never had such credit been given to the evolution of the human race and to living species in general, and all with the enthusiastic approval of the « in-house intellectuals » who occupied the seats of learning, and who moulded the thinking of those who would subsequently occupy them. Then, as we know, the spell was broken: the liberist cycle and the implosion of the USSR brought the castle of « avant-garde thinking » tumbling down. The western in-house intellectuals recycled themselves from lead dancers in the ballet of nationalist socialism to standard-bearers of « peaceful and pacifist » imperialist democracy.
Socialism had been born by magic, and by magic it vanished. Moscow and Tirana, Bucharest and Prague, are no longer socialist. Peking survives, but poses a few problems of defi-

Europe's historic tendency towards unification was thus blocked by a gangsters' deal: « *The truth about unitary imperialism is that Europe as presently constituted is the outcome of a gangsters' deal that apportioned spheres of influence, following the defeat of a Nazi Germany that had attempted to unify and to dominate the entire continent with blood and iron. Roosevelt and Stalin agreed to divide what Hitler had been unable to unite, and by raising the flags of democracy and of socialism, completed the hellish dynamic of the European war* ».[54]

nition for the now elderly « in-house intellectuals ». Could it be that « socialist » Peking is now entering some odd transitional state? What about West Bengal, where government socialism has been in power for some time – could it be entering its final phase, and how will it maintain a position undermined by the social changes that have shaken India?
Clearly, these continue to be real problems for a decreasing number of « in-house intellectuals » a number which, to be honest, is at risk of extinction. At this point an observation on the evolution of the species may be appropriate. Throughout the centuries, we have established the evolution of ape to man, excluding the possibility of a regression from man to ape.
The theoretical formula « socialism in one country » has demonstrated that the regression from man to ape, at any rate among opportunist theoreticians, is a legacy of our species.
It hasn't taken long for the nature of the evolution – or better, the involution – of opportunist thinking, that whole bazaar of spells and illusions, to be exposed. With the « financial crisis » the State has come back to haunt the « back alleys of interventionism ».
The USA sets the style, even if a bit chaotically. The grandchildren of the « in-house intellectuals », now themselves the intellectuals of the official or backbench parliamentary left wing, are racking their brains: has socialism sprung up in America? If it's not socialism, is it « progressive interventionism » or « interventionist liberism » or « capitalism with a good measure of collectivism »? But only one real doubt remains: in the age of imperialism, are there any limits to the involution of opportunist thinking? From ape, is it possible to regress to fish?

Two apparently opposing camps put themselves forward, one as defender of « democracy and freedom », the other as « socialism achieved »: but the voice of the proletariat is absent, and it finds itself pressed into the service of one side or the other: « *It wasn't the first time that the victors had divided the spoils between them. It was the first time that one of the biggest and most brutal imperialist episodes of robbery and plunder produced such an enormous mass ideology to justify and glorify itself. The international proletariat paid a high price in terms of its moral bondage, and in its theoretical, political and organisational loss of autonomy. It has paid, and will go on paying, until such time as State capitalism continues to oppress the working class in the name of Communism.*

The Yalta agreement was imposed with force and was accepted by a public consensus previously assured by propaganda. The few internationalists who did not accept the Pax Unitary Imperialism were eliminated. The jury of history is still out on the role played by the internationalist movement. Yalta was the nadir of internationalism».[55]

Imperialist democracy: an illusion and a fraud

Democracy is a word that derives from the Greek and means *government by the people*. The term has been in use since the time of Ancient Greece, but within different historical contexts *the people* has had widely varying meanings, and for this reason, *democracy* should always be used with a specific explanatory adjective.

In the slave-owning society in which the term sprang up, for example, *the people* were the totality of free citizens, for whom democracy was in fact a government of slave-owners: it was a *slave-owning democracy*.

Similarly, the most widespread system is today *imperialist democracy*, the form of government that best guarantees imperialism control over the wage-earning slaves of modern times.

The crisis of parliamentarianism is increasingly making clear that real power does not reside in the representative structures of *democracy*: «*the financial oligarchy imports and exports capital, concentrates, merges and sells industrial complexes at international or at least at European level, independently of all the anti-trust laws of the anti-monopoly parliamentary commissions*».[56]

On a theoretical level, this «*gradual emptying of content*» is explained by the process of political centralisation that corresponds to the concentration of the means of production. In *Imperialism*, Lenin defines the traits of a « *share-holding democracy* » underlining how an increase in numbers of share-holders corresponds to a real increase in the power of capitalists « *and their opportunities to manipulate the sleaziest transactions* »: « *Millions of bank notes give their millions of individual owners simply the economic power of a limited and circumscribed purchasing capacity: when centralised in a bank, this money gives the bank owners immense economic power which is not diminished and indeed is increased by the individual depositors' unceasing right to their money* ».[57]

The share-holding system corresponds to the system of political participation: if the possession of one share carries the entitlement of one vote, in politics there is the corresponding principle of « *one man, one vote* ». A single vote confers no real political power, just as there is no real power in owning one share in Microsoft or Volkswagen, but the illusion that all members of society are equal persists. In certain phases of history, the ruling class has been forced to rely on authoritarian or Fascist forms of government, but the « *best shell* » for its control remains democracy, and it is reinstated as soon as possible.

The democratic system also provides for the spreading of the illusion that exercising the parliamentary vote can change society. Lenin had early warned against treating electoral struggles as a superior form of political action: « *Nothing in our times can be done without elections; nothing can be done without the masses. And in this era of printing and parliamentarianism it is impossible to gain the following of the masses without a widely ramified, systematically managed, well-equipped system of flattery, lies, fraud, juggling with fashionable and popular catchwords and promising all manner of reforms and blessings to the workers right and left – as long as they renounce the revolutionary struggle for the overthrow of the bourgeoisie* ».[58]

In contemporary society, the disease has now spread everywhere, and the more the *honourable assemblies* are relegated to the role of mere executors of decisions taken in the centres of financial power, the more their members imagine that their debates – increasingly uttered in deserted halls – are decisive: unless they are obediently falling into line and presenting a united front when the ruling class calls them to order.

Chapter 3

The New Strategic Phase

« *Dialectics calls for a many-sided investigation into a given social phenomenon in its development, and for the external and the seeming to be reduced to the fundamental motive forces, to the development of the productive forces, and to the class struggle* ».

Lenin, *The Collapse of the Second International*
Chap.III
Written in May/June 1915 and published in the same year in the journal "Kommunist" No. 1-2

The first clear signal of the changes accompanying the great developments of the post Second World War period was the restructuring of the mid 1970s, at the beginning of the liberist cycle. By then, capitalism was triumphant throughout the world, and this triumph took the ideological form of glorifying the free market.

These economic changes took years to come to fruition, before suddenly bringing into question the balance of relationships between the powers.

At the end of the 1980s, history accelerated, with the lightning reunification of Germany, the implosion of the USSR – drained by the *Star Wars* rearmament race and financially weakened by the fall in petrol prices – and the sudden collapse of its empire: all taking place between November 1989 and December 1991. The effect on relations between the powers was the equivalent of a third world war.

Everything speeded up: « *Today history has unexpectedly quickened its step. This is a phenomenon that can only be understood via historic materialism. An analysis of the 1500s, itself a century of acceleration and of a break with the past, is a model for the Marxist vision: Europe takes off, Asia loses ground, remaining the continent of a hundred thousand villages and of despotism, America makes it's entry into civilisation. Modern history is born. Today, four events characterise the runaway course of world imperialism: the end of Yalta, the lightning reunification of Germany, the breakdown of the USSR, and the Gulf War. The interweaving of these processes, and the new divisions they produce, weigh in the scales of history like a third world war, the outcome of which cannot be foreseen* ».[59]

The disappearance of the supposed *socialist camp* wrong-footed the political heirs of Stalinism, who had to quickly recycle themselves on the political scene.

Europe's opportunity was the vigorous resumption of the process of European unification: « *The end of Yalta has unfrozen the European order that emerged from the Second Imperialist Conflict, and which aimed to prevent Germany rising again as a dominant power in Europe, since such a power would not have stopped at the borders of the Old Continent. The lightning unification of Germany has created a power with around 80 million of a population, with a decisive economic significance for both east and west Europe* ».[60]

The process of European unification was rendered more urgent by capitalist development in Asia and primarily in China and India, which forced European big business to expand and merge its markets, in order to be able to compete with rivals of continental dimensions.

This process has been going on for a number of years: the *Treaty of Rome*, which set up the *European Economic Community*, was signed in 1957, but there has been a sudden and very marked acceleration. In 1992, the basis for monetary unification was laid at *Maastricht*: in 1995 the *Schengen* convention freed up the movement of labour within the borders of the European Union, subjecting such movement to a single set of laws without regard to national frontiers. The first day of January 2002 saw the debut of the euro, which apart from representing the unification of monetary power, has also had a great ideological impact on the masses, because of its effects on daily life.

It was not, of course, an easy process, because the objective economic interests of the big business groups that would be promoted by unification met resistance from different political and cultural traditions capable of halting and obstructing the process: periods of *stop-go* bore witness to the difficulties of building unified political structures. Nor was it a peaceful process, although European imperialism continues to put itself forward as a «*peaceful power*»: in a continent that for centuries has been torn apart by bloody wars, and which last century was the scene of two world wars, it is easy enough to present the union of all European peoples as a step towards peace.

«*For centuries Europe has been an idea, holding out hope of peace and understanding. That hope has been fulfilled. European unification has made peace and prosperity possible. It has bought about a sense of community and overcome differences (...) European unification shows that we have learnt the painful lessons of a history marked by bloody conflict*» states the official document approved for the fiftieth anniversary of the *Treaty of Rome.*

The ideological deal is easy, but it distorts reality. For a start, the wars in the *former Yugoslavia* were really wars of European unification, marked by the conflict between the European markets and the resistance of Russian imperialism attempting to defend its sphere of influence: « *We have already refuted that the implosion of the USSR could be considered peaceful, given a balance of between three hundred thousand and half a million dead in the succession of wars that accompanied the break with the past between 1989 and 1991. If anything, those conflicts have now been consigned to the history of imperialism, not just as the result of the implosion of Russia and Yugoslavia, and as heradling German reunification, but as wars of European unification*».[61]

This distortion affects not only the past, but also the future. European imperialism has united in order to be able to bear the clash with other world powers: today we hear the voices of the forces of production, of international commerce, of finance, but tomorrow the guns and the armies will speak: «*If the need for a common defence really does drive war from its heart on the Rhine, it will be to drive it elsewhere, into the generator of global tensions that the selfsame birth of the European Union will help to produce and stoke up. If it manages to centralise the political violence of states that have fought each other for centuries, it will draw power to itself, but only to unleash violence in its turn in a clash of imperialist powers*».[62]

As in the time of Lenin, today the true internationalists are those who fight against their home-grown imperialism: today, more than ever before, «*the enemy is in our own house*» even more so when the enemy wears the winning mask of a *benign* power.

Meanwhile, in Asia, an economic development without precedent is taking place. *Unequal development* has meant that China, at the beginning of the 1900s still partitioned by the imperialist powers, can today join the gang of thieves who divide the world market between them.

In the course of a century, China has kept the same share of world population (around 20 %) but a consistent share of that immense population is progressively becoming part of the proletariat and producing surplus value: it is estimated that every year 1 % of the Chinese population moves from the countryside and joins the urban working class.

India, Brasil, even Russia, once more lifting its head – other world giants are complicating the multipolar power game, taking advantage of the relative decline of the older powers. If European imperialism can play against its decline on the field of economic, political and military union, and by acquiring eastern Europe's *reservoirs of surplus value*, the USA must follow other paths.

In 1945 the USA was the dominant power, responsible for one half of world production: today the situation is very different. The *twin deficit* phenomenon – a huge public debt largely financed by selling government bonds for foreign capital, and a major trade imbalance in relation to China: growing competition from the Asian giants: and a European unification that has produced a fearsome rival for the dollar – have all speeded up American decline.

The crisis in global relations triggered by the collapse of the *sub-prime* mortgage market has highlighted a situation that has long been critical: « *The crisis not only disclosed, but has highlighted, relations between large areas of the world market. America has been living on credit, financing part of its consumption by importing cheap goods from the emerging areas, while its financial centre, New York, recycles capital from Asia and from the oil-producing countries* ».[63]

In 2003 came the « *war of choice* » against Iraq: « *the warning light of the general nature of the contention was the outbreak of war in Iraq, with its revelation of relations within the balance of power. The conflict was on the scale of a "small war", but it demonstrated that the global balance needed to be regulated – by that "political war" declared by Washington. This is why it could already be observed that it would not be surprising if the war were reflected "in a new balance between the main economic areas and globalisation", even if this did not yet compromise the liberist nature of the cycle. This conflict was the sign that the balance between protectionism and liberism was in transformation* ».[64]

That war produced a savage balance-sheet, and one not yet finalised: « *up to 100,000 Iraqi dead, more than 4,000 dead between USA and coalition troops, three and a half million refugees and displaced persons. Karl Marx explains that in a capitalist society, goods are a fetish that conceal relations between the people who have produced them (...) So: a tankful of petrol appears to be just a tankful of petrol. Yet for five years the war fought around the Iraqi oil fields has produced at least fifty dead per day. They should be calculated into the average price of petrol at the pump* ».[65]

There are other costs in calculating the price of the struggle with time: the time of the rise of the Asian powers, the time of the European unification process, the time of American decline. Into this struggle breaks the crisis: « *The financial catastrophe is a watershed, definitively demonstrating that the nature of the crisis is one of global relations. The collapse of the credit banks has also swept away the smokescreen that for a time appeared to limit the crisis to "phoney money" and the bursting of the property bubble. The erosion of American power – a power for long bound up with a dependence on international capital – is not only suddenly exposed, but is also exacerbated* ».[66]

Imperialism has not changed since Lenin's time: war is still *the continuation of politics by violent means*: there are still *generations of young people destroyed by war* (we need only consider that the number of American military personnel who commit suicide after returning from Iraq is higher than the number fallen in battle): and international organisations are still powerless, or connive with the powerful.

And still crisis devastates the world, striking directly at the conditions of life of the masses. We have reached the point, as Marx would say, at which *the development of the productive forces comes into conflict with the existing relations of production.*

For now, the crisis has not transformed the liberist brand name of the economic cycle, but all the evidence points to capitalism having had its day, and that the conditions for social revolution and progress to a better form of social organisation are coming to fruition.

But historical experience poses a disturbing question: will the revolutionary movement be equal to the situation? Will there be a Leninist party capable of understanding and action?

« *Marxism analyses the long cycle in order to pinpoint the fault lines and the unstoppable engine of uneven economic and political growth, in order not to fall into fatalism or a lazy repetition of a matter of principle. Marxism becomes the science-party only if it carries out that task* ». In the storms of history, there is no middle way: « *Either win over politically every individual addressed in the struggle against imperialism – and thus against the real forms that its ideologies and political currents assume – or it will be imperialism to do this, without this even being perceived, because the ideologies and the currents of imperialism will be the very air breathed by the common perception, the false consciousness of the age that permeates every aspect of social psychology* ».[67]

Today the Leninist party exists: throughout previous decades, a scientific laboratory and an organisational legacy has been laboriously rebuilt. We will see how today Marxist science is capable of understanding the changes of the new strategic phase – modern imperialist development, how a multiplicity of crises present themselves, the progress of the new robber bands, and the extraordinary growth of the world proletariat.

A quick sketch will help define the practical tasks, to plan revolutionary activity, and to act: « *In this, the strategic perspective of the long cycle is the opposite of passive waiting, or of the myth that revolution is inevitable. It must be capable of being translated into today's practical political struggle, so as to contrast the influence of the ruling ideology step by step* ».[68]

Understanding the present

A cycle of unrepeatable development

When the killing was over and the spoils of the vanquished had been divided up, the economy of the post Second World War period began to drive forward again: in the first 30 years, according to the calculations of Angus Maddison, the Gross World Product (GWP) tripled, but uneven development was immediately evident.

The USA increased its Gross Domestic Product (GDP) by 2.4: Asia by 4.2 (but Japan by 7.9, India by 2.4 and China by 3.2): western Europe by 3 (but Germany by 3.6, France by 3.2, Italy by 3.6, Great Britain by 1.9): Latin America by 4.3 and the USSR by 3. As soon as a balance of forces was established, the differing paces of change promised to throw it into dispute.

Cervetto summarises the changes between the powers thus: « *(...)the crucial years for America's downsizing were the late 1960s (...) western Europe peaked in 1970 (...) the 1960s were therefore the years in which the big business groups of imperialist Europe re-emerged (...) Basically, the points the United States lost were picked up by Japan, since even the USSR (...) had not made much of an impact as regards its share of world product, because it too had recently undergone a retrenchment* ».[69]

In the following 30 years, the Gross World Product tripled again, but the imbalances in growth were even more evident: India doubled its percentage of GWP, while China quadrupled it. Between 1975 and 2003, Asia as a continent went from 24.9 % to 40.5 % of GWP. In relation to these figures, the USA fell back, while Europe forged ahead thanks to its annexation of eastern Europe.

Development has become more uneven in the last fifteen years.

«*According to World Trade Organisation data, from 1900 to 2000 China went from 1.9 % to 4.7 % of world export of manufactured goods, gaining just over 0.25 % a year. From 2000 to 2006 it more than doubled its share, reaching 10.8 % at the amazing rate of one percentage point increase per year. Excluding trade within the EU-25, in 2006 Europe exported manufactured goods to the tune of 1,234 billion dollars, equal to 21 % of the total: China 895 billion, equal to 15 %: the US 829 billion, equal to 14 %: and Japan 587 billion, equal to 10 %. In fifteen years, Beijing has become the world's second-biggest exporting power in the manufacturing sector, generating, according to how this is calculated, from one-tenth to one-seventh of world exports. In the last few years, this has occurred at three times the speed of the previous decade: a real breakthrough, made possible by China's entry into the WTO*».[70]

From the post-war period till today, we have seen a truly *unrepeatable* cycle of capitalist development at world level: *unrepeatable* because in 1945 two-thirds of the world's population, in the countries of Asia, were living in economically and culturally backward societies, while today this has been reduced to about one-third.

The last is a forecast for stormy weather: on the one hand, space for future expansion is reducing, while on the other hand we are seeing a growing imbalance in the relative strengths of the big powers. This is not yet at breaking point – the breakdown of order point – but it is only a matter of time: the time required for the growth of the new powers.

We have already, however, entered an age in which the relations between powers will be sorely tested: witness the acute nature of the *crisis of global relations* triggered by the bursting of the house price bubble.

Imperialism, which has already caused two world wars, has not changed: only the scale of its development, and therefore of its contradictions, is different. This can be understood by observing the formation of ever-growing conglomerates.

In Book 3 of *Capital*, when Marx summarises the « three fundamental characteristics » of capitalism, he places alongside the *socialisation of labour* and the *creation of a world market* the *concentration of the means of production*. This *concentration*, which is actually an *expropriation* because it deprives a large section of small producers of their means, forcing them to become wage labourers – «*is accomplished by the action of the immanent laws of capitalist production itself, by the centralisation of capital. One capitalist always kills many others*».[71]

Studying capitalism in his time, Lenin realised that Marx's forecasts had been amply verified, and that the process of capital concentration at a world level had reached the stage of *forming monopolies with decisive economic functions.* This process continues today, the extensive development of capitalism itself enforcing capital concentration at ever-higher levels.

The news provides us with a thousand demonstrations of this reality. For example, delivery services. In place of the old national postal services, there are now «*highly technological transport logistics and delivery centres*» themselves in the process of merging, in response to increases in the price of fuel and transport. UPS, the world's biggest group, gives some idea of the industry's dimension: it employs 425,000 people and shifts nearly 16 million parcels all over the world every day. The leader in Europe is TNT, with 121,000 employees in 200 countries.

Another example: beer is a rapidly expanding market, (especially in China). «*Between 2001 and 2006 world sales of beer increased by 273.9 hectolitres of which 119 went to Peking and the surrounding area*» according to *l'Espresso* on 31/7/08. The growth of this market has over the same period been responsible for more than 150 takeovers and mergers among the big world groups, ending by making this sector one of the most concentrated. The largest takeover was by *InBev*, the biggest world group, which owns Belgium's *Stella Artois*, *Leffe,* and *Hoegaarden*: Germany's *Becks*, Brasil's *Brama, Anctartica,* and *Skol*, Czechoslovakia's *Staropramen*, Argentina's *Quilmes*, China's *Sedrin*, and Britain's *Tennents*. By taking over Canada's *Labatt* from the American firm *Budweiser*, the second-largest world group, *InBev* now controls around three hundred brands.

A group that projects a *young*, attractive image, and a *low-cost* sales strategy is *IKEA*. Founded in 1943 by the Swede Ingvar Kampred (whose *Testament of a furniture salesman* is still given out to new employees) today the firm has a permanent workforce of 104,000, spread over 32 factories and 230 sales points. In reality, more than 104,000 people work for IKEA: another 100,000 in India alone, while the biggest share of production is carried out in China. IKEA was born in Sweden, but where is its *national base* now? The producers are in 54 different countries, the sales points are in 44: the patents and the know-how, which constitute the firm's real income, are held by *IKEA service*, which is controlled by another society with its seat, says *Le Monde*, *« in that fiscal paradise, the Caribbean »*.[72]

The process of forming ever-larger groups that concentrate enormous sums of capital and an immense labour force has reached levels never previously known. *Mediobanca's* 2007 report on *Research and Development* documents how 342 big multi-nationals employ 26 million of the world's people: 147 of these multi-nationals are in Europe, 66 in the USA-Canada, 50 in Russia and Asia, and 34 in Japan.

If we then consider the economic importance of these firms, we realise how some big business groups have more economic weight than whole States: *Toyota* is more or less equivalent to the Gross Domestic Product of Greece, Russia's *Gazprom* is worth more than Iran's GDP, and *Volkswagen* is nearly equivalent in value to the GDP of Venezuela. These groups, therefore, are of such a size that in their inevitable clashes they are able to influence the policies and politics of States.

The role of the State, the distillation of the violence of the imperialist era, becomes essential. Today it is presented as a novelty, after years during which the globalisation myth reigned supreme due to the high pace of world market development, frequently exemplified by the worldwide spread of the big international groups. With its goods and capital, the bourgeoisie had demolished every « *Great Wall of China* », and, it was said, more or less the role of the state.

The awakening was sharp. The salvage operations and the nationalisation of the big financial groups demonstrate the failure of these ideologies.

« *The liberist religion of the "rational market" is on its knees, but not all its high priests, who, on the contrary, are supervising the new distribution of bread and wine – state and market – in the liturgy of the new strategic phase. This is no surprise for Marxist theory. If the State is the tool of the ruling class, the bourgeoisie has never ceased to use it on the domestic and international markets, despite brandishing the "state question" in the struggles among its various factions, and in the confrontations between rival bourgeois states, or even in its own case, when it works – as Hegel would say – for itself rather than in itself* ».[73]

In the debate on the crisis, the Chinese *Moloch* is described as ready to cast its shadow and get its hands on the world, from Africa to Central America. A bit much for our internationalist concepts to be so favoured now, in the middle of all this mess.

The financial Tower of Babel

Among the features Lenin lists as marking out imperialism, is *the merging of banking capital with industrial capital and the creation, on this base, of « finance capital », of a financial oligarchy, and the great importance given to the export of capital in relation to the export of goods.* On the one hand, the capital in the banks, (which Marx defines as *the representatives of all who lend money*) had immediately become the property of industrial enterprises: on the other hand, credit mechanisms had become complicated in the interests of increasingly centralising capital for investment.

Today that process has moved further ahead, creating a real *Tower of Babel* of operations and of financial products that seem to have *a life of their own* in relation to the original aim of capital centralisation, to the point of being able to give the illusion that wealth can be created by speculation and not by the process of production.

In its essence, the phenomenon had already been described by Marx, who, dealing in Book III of *Capital* with *fictitious capital*, wrote: « *It is the object of banking to give facilities to trade, and whatever gives facilities to trade gives facilities to speculation. Trade and speculation are in some cases so nearly allied that it is impossible to say at what precise point trade ends and speculation begins* ».[74] but what has changed today is the size of the phenomenon.

« *Abundant world savings have created the magic of leverage – the possibility of making an investment, covering a small percentage of it with one's capital and the rest with bank loans (...) At the beginning of 2007, the London think tank Independent Strategy made a sketch of the global "liquidity pyramid": currency and the reserves of the central banks (power money) amounted to 10 % of world GDP: the liquidity resulting from bank loans (broad money) accounted for 130 % of GDP: while structured debt and derivatives totalled a figurative value of 800 % of world GP. The base of the pyramid had quintupled in the first years of the present decade. Bank loans in the USA exceeded the world average. George Magnus, an economist at UBS, has estimated the evolution of US "credit intensity": in the 1950s, for every dollar growth in GDP, a dollar and a half in credit was generated: in the 1990s, this ratio had doubled: in 2007, credit had reached 4.5 dollars for every additional dollar of GDP* ».[75]

Every so often, a floor of this enormous Tower of Babel collapses, causing losses for speculators, who regularly talk of: « *"burning wealth" but this "wealth" is mostly paper money, which feeds the illusion of its own durability, along with the gamble that tomorrow it will be worth more* ».[76]

It is wealth on *paper*, although naturally the investors who believed in the possibility of easy gains suffer real losses: moreover, given the existence of such a strong tie between the world of production and the world of finance, it is practically impossible for a financial crisis not to have more or less serious effects on the real economy.

In this sense, the American *subprime* crisis of 2007 has been a model crisis. When the crisis broke in July 2007, it: « *is one of the least surprising ones in living memory. To our great satisfaction, our newspaper has always trusted in the steady beam of scientific Marxism to illuminate the mysteries of capital: we had already spoken of the "bubble" in the autumn of 2005, quoting, among others, IMF sources and evaluations dating back to 2003 and 2004. The truth is that the "house price bubble" started to swell immediately after the collapse of the previous speculative wave, the dotcom bubble, and the one was largely the result and continuation of the other* ».[77] An investment in property appeared, by definition, to be a safe investment.

« *Promoting the solidity of bricks and mortar, house agents and mortgage banks cast their nets among low and medium-low income-earners, to awaken in them the dream of becoming homeowners. Subprime mortgages for would-be home owners with poor credit ratings, little capital to make a down payment, and willing to pay over half their income into a mortgage, mushroomed. (...) In 2006 alone, three million mortgages were taken out, 630,000 of them subprime* ».[78] A cut in fiscal pressure, cheap goods from Asia that kept inflation down, and the influx of Chinese capital, buying American Treasury bonds and financing the federal deficit, allowed loans to be made at good rates of interest, even to *subprime* customers offering security inferior to the *prime* average.

When the trend of rising house prices ended, and prices started to fall, it was a disaster: mortgages were no longer secured by real estate values, repayments on variable interest mortgages rose, and millions of homeowners lost their house. But the crisis spread throughout the world of finance because: « *The mortgage bank offloads the risk of subprime mortgages onto Wall Streets's funds and banks; in their turn, they break them up and transform them into securities, mixing them with others in such mouth-watering combinations as to tempt even the most jaded palates: the rating agencies give the securities, which are then sold on the international markets, a respectable, often AAA rating* ».[79]

Now *leverage* worked in reverse: every real dollar lost was multiplied in the mechanisms of international

A memorable storm

The crisis that began in July 2007 with the bursting of the subprime bubble culminated in September 2008 with the Wall Street crash: « *Wall Street has collapsed, lashed by a storm that will go down in history. Washington is struggling to get its bearings, debating an extraordinary State intervention equal to about a tenth of the national product. London has also been dragged into the eye of the hurricane: Middle Europe is weighing up its influence on negotiations and support to the USA, but it too has been affected by the crisis. Asia is relying on the importance of its sovereign funds, vast reserves accumulated through export, but it too will suffer a reduction in international trade. The truth is that no one can yet calculate just how severe the global crisis will become, but it is sure to change the power relations between America, Asia and Europe. An ideology thirty years old is crumbling: imperialist liberism is in doubt. The Old Continent believes it has the advantage of measures inherited from market social economy: it has never entirely abandoned regulation and the hand of the public sector. The ideologies of opportunism and parliamentarianism have always represented State intervention as progress and social justice. No surprises there: public finance is the natural element of such ideologies, and for a long time even the ideology of USSR statism was regarded fondly. A new political cycle is beginning: economists, columnists, parliamentarians and*

finance, causing banks to fail, with the loss of related jobs. But the world of the real economy was also hit: fewer new houses were built (the first firm to report notable losses was *Caterpillar*): the furniture and furnishing sector went into crisis: demand for transport of goods fell: in this difficult situation, millions of families reduced their consumption. All this in the face of the complete impotence of the principal authorities on the world economy to foresee, prevent, or remedy. One year after the subprime crisis, financial crises and slowdown of the cycle intertwine with exceptional events that force the governments of the powers to intervene.

« *With the nationalisation on September 7*th *of the two home loan giants Freddie Mac and Fannie Mae, the financial crisis in the United States has taken a great leap forwards, both in nature and intensity. In roughly ten days the face of US finance has changed: two leaders will dance attendance on the rediscovery of the public good. So it may be as well to recall how this rediscovery began: thousands of billions of dollars and euros, consigned by emergency plans and special powers to prop up the commercial bankers' gambles. To put it bluntly – the State as the tool of Capital. A memory for the future*».[80]

State intervention in an attempt to limit the effects of the crisis does not immediately mean a change in the liberist sign of the cycle, still less a «reformation» in the future workings of the free market. On the contrary: in the United States, a crucial front: «*in which the Treasury secretary is concentrating his artillery, is that of the capital markets: their openness must be guaranteed at all costs and against every protectionist temptation. Their international dimensions were decisive not only in the Freddie-Fannie rescue, but also in that of AIG, present in 130 countries, long linked with China, and tied to European banks by big insurance contracts. Paulson wanted to include the major foreign banks present in the USA in his Wall Street rescue. For the former CEO of Goldman Sachs, "saving the market by itself" has no odour of repentance. It is the indispensable condition for keeping the US power, though wounded and doped with strong injections of newly-issued dollars, on all the fronts of the imperialist contention. It is an arduous task to have palingenesis without an apocalypse. These are dramatic times for capitalism. These are crucial times for scientific communism, and fertile times for the organisation of the working class*».[81]

American investment banks Lehman Brothers and Merrill Lynch, have left the scene, the former ending its 150-year history before the bankruptcy judge, the latter – almost 100 years old – being taken over by Bank of America for 50 billion dollars. Morgan Stanley and Goldman Sachs, under fire in the stock exchanges, have had to shore up their capital, the first entering into partnership with the Japanese financial group Mitsubishi UFJ, and the second with the US financier Warren Buffet. The top US insurance group, American International Group (AIG) has been nationalised, and the top savings bank, Washington Mutual, has been absorbed by JP Morgan.

The federal list of the bank deposit insurance agency lists 117 banks at risk. On the other shore of the Atlantic, the leading British building society, HBOS, has been taken over by Lloyds TSB, with the active support of the Labour government. "Bank amalgamation" is on the agenda in all the metropolises.

The collapse of the superpower's hallowed temples is spreading fear and pulverising the credibility of the financial system. Stock exchanges from New York to Moscow, from London to Hong Kong, from Paris to Shanghai, and from Milan to Delhi, Seoul, or Tokyo are "panic-stricken"».[82]

The crisis is an exemplary model, especially for the way it has thrown into sharp relief relations between the great areas of the world market, presenting as «*the first battle of a new war, in which America and Europe confront emerging China*». And China's financial strength was immediately demonstrated by its assault on the main western banks in difficulty (in the guise of rescue by the investment of «*sovereign funds*» – owned by the Chinese state), thus further increasing international connections between big business groups. While: «*The United States is in the midst of a political crisis, combined with an economic crisis whose precedent can only be found in the 1930s. Shifts in global relations are maturing, the effects of which will be felt for years to come. This means that strategic reflection needs to return to the basis of the Marxist theory of international relations*».[83]

A long battle to realign the superstructures of imperialism has begun: a battle that cannot be waged without taking the new rising powers into consideration, although in the imperialist dialectic of unity/division, the sign of unity prevails. For now.

Just one battle today then, but a battle heralding tomorrow's inevitable war.

Imperialist hunger

Marxism holds that the objective of capitalist production is not to meet need, but to valorize capital: in other words, there is food on the table not because we are hungry, but because the production and sale of food guarantees a profit. There is no other explanation for how it is possible for part of the human race to go hungry while another part eats too much.

And yet: « *We thought we were heading for a solution – if not for poverty, at least for the problem of starvation: certainly, there are still a billion malnourished people in the world, but in the 15 years from 1900 to the middle of this decade, their number fell by a good 278 million. A positive trend that seemed destined to continue: (but today) in Africa, Asia and Latin America, 36 countries are at risk of civil war. They are extremely poor nations, in which people spend more than half their income – often two-thirds – on food. In many cases – from Haiti to Kenya – serious and bloody revolts have broken out* ».[84]

This situation is not due to natural catastrophes, but to the dynamic of prices that make food available on the market, but not available to those whose income is too low: « *The explosive rise in the cost of living is increasing the suffering of those strata of the world population that allocate half or more of their incomes for food (...) The World Bank reports that over one billion human beings live on less than one dollar a day, and another billion and a half on an income ranging from one to two dollars, while 850 million suffer from acute, chronic hunger* ».[85]

There is no doubt that food is produced in abundance: according to the FAO, world stocks of cereal total 405 million tons, bringing stocks available for 2008 to 16 % higher than demand: « *in fact, the quantity of food produced in the world is sufficient to feed the population of the world. But studies on hunger and malnutrition point up the issue of actual access to food* » as Simona Beretta reminds us in the *Osservatore Romano* of 24th August 2008.

Speculation is surely one factor, influencing the price of food as it influences any other market product. Those who were selling rice at 400 dollars per ton at the end of 2007 realised that if they delayed selling they would gain much more: by March 2008 it had sprung up to 800 dollars per ton, which became 1000 in May, with the trend still upwards. The truth is that considering rice is the basic food of half the human race, in practice this sort of speculation condemns a number of people to death: but the profits are realised in the Stock Exchanges of New

York or Hong Kong, while the starving are thousands of miles away.

The profits go to the big food distributors and agro-chemical suppliers, from *Wal-Mart* (USA) to *Nestlè*, from the *Potash Corporation* (Canada) to *K+S* (Germany), *Sinochem* (China) and so on. Some investment funds, to recoup their *subprime* losses, have even thrown themselves into stock market, gambling on future food price rises: one example is *Calpers*, the pension fund for California's public sector workers, and standard-bearer of « *socially responsible* » investment.

But speculation is not the only factor. The rise in prices also results from the growth of the Asian market, and the consequent *westernisation* of consumption.

« *"The Economist" recalls that the consumption of cereals is linked to demography, while that of meat is tied to economic growth. This shift is one aspect of the change in the balance of power, and at the same time in the balance of the classes within the emerging countries, through urbanisation and the transformation of agriculture. In the last twenty years, the Chinese have increased their per capita consumption of meat from 20 to 50 kilograms per year, absorbing, according to the IMF, from 35 % to 40 % of the increase in global consumption. In no way does this reduce the demand for cereals, because animals bred for slaughter are great consumers of these: it takes three kilograms of cereals to produce one kilo of pork, and eight for one kilo of beef (...) The higher demand along the whole meat production chain increases both price and transport costs, since it is not the local markets that satisfy this demand* ».[86]

In short, the logic of profit creates a paradoxical situation: although we have an *excess of production over consumption*, the number of people in the world suffering from hunger is increasing, because of *economic development*.

Completing the scenario is the choice of many big groups to throw themselves into the production of *bio-fuel* based on cereals – a giant business involving such big groups as *General Electric, BP, Shell*, and the agricultural colossus *Cargill.*

« Those who play down the importance of bio-fuels observe that they account for a mere 1.3 % of total oil consumption, while those who criticise them – the World Bank, for example – observe that between 2004 and 2007 US bio-fuels, to the detriment of food, absorbed the entire increase in the global production of maize. Other international organisations – IMF, FAO (Food and Agriculture Organisation), IFPRI (International Food Policy Research Institute) – estimate that they account for a 10-30 % increase in food prices (...). The debate is fuelled not only by economic and domestic political calculations, but also by relations between the metropolises and the big oil-producing countries or petrostates, hostile to bio-fuels ».[87]

This should please the environmentalists: after demanding the production of more *ecological* fuel, they now see that in order to sow profitable plantations of soya and cereals, wide tracts of virgin forest in the Amazon, China and Borneo are being burnt down.

Moreover, the World Bank warns that: «*A tankful of ethanol would feed one person for a whole year (...) The crisis demonstrates that the double nature of imperialist development, which increases the forces of production only to destroy them in the wars and chaos of capitalism, operates in the same way on human beings*». The FAO speaks of 100 million people having fallen into the category of malnourished, because of the food price crisis. «*A conservative estimate suggests that the falling back of these 100 million into poverty would bring to 500-700 thousand the individuals who would pay the price of capitalist hunger. This is the additional human cost of a war*».[88]

But a system based on profit certainly can't take account of that.

The new Molochs of imperialism

During the post-war period, nearly everyone took it for granted that China was a socialist country. To maintain that it was only a country of state capitalism, as was our political line in those years, seemed heresy. « *We have been following the development of Chinese state capitalism since the 1950s, well before European intellectuals became infatuated with Mao Zedong, and without falling into their childish self-illusions: it was a young capitalism that was growing in China, certainly not an impossible national socialism. We have studied the great imperialist leap that, in fifteen years, has allowed China to become the second manufacturing exporter in the world, filling its coffers with dollar currency reserves* ».[89]

Today it is clear that the country which was labelled *the greatest socialist country in the world* by the unready intellectuals of the Left is on the way to becoming *the greatest imperialist country in the world.*

« *This encirclement of the old metropolises was never imagined by those petit-bourgeois intellectuals who grew out of adolescence clutching Mao's Little Red Book: those same intellectuals now growing old in the sinecures of bourgeois newspapers, of state and private television companies, of the transformist political parties of both Left and Right. They dreamt of a papier-maché China, made by children playing together on the landing. And now China is here, with its products and its wage levels* ».[90]

All available studies document the development of China: according to one – the annual report on technological development published in 2008 by the *Georgia Institute of Technology*, China has become the number one exporter of high-technology products. According to the index employed by this study, China has moved from a value of 20.7 in 1993 to 82.8 in 2007, while in the same period the USA has gone from a value of 90 to 76.1. This outcome is thought to be due to the dynamic of « the relationship between investments » in « research and development » and China's Gross Domestic Product (one of the highest in the world): to the interaction between local industry and the research centres established in China by multinationals from all over the world: and to the special attention paid to the training of qualified technicians (a million graduates in science and engineering every year).

The *Georgia Institute* has produced a timely analysis of the process, beginning with a study of the Special

Economic Zones, where western industry was encouraged by fiscal exemptions and a free hand in managing both economic enterprise and workforce: « *These are the regions (...) where we find the biggest cities, the greatest population density, and the highest rates of growth for the industrial workforce. Therefore, they are the Mecca of internal migrations that could without exaggeration be described as biblical, if the figures reported by the international media are even close to the truth: the population in transit, the "mang liu", amount to 80 million according to Business Week, 60-70 million according to a French analysis* ».[91]

These statistics record the transformation of millions of peasant farmers into proletarians, into producers of surplus value.

A typical example: Shenzen (where one of the first SEZs was set up) had by 1994 grown from a fishing village to a *metropolis of two and a half million* inhabitants. By 2008 this figure had grown to 10 million, with an urban area that will soon spread to merge with Hong Kong.

Today China is one of the main imperialist powers of the world, with a gigantic productive potential (it is known as *the workshop of the world*), one trillion dollars worth of currency reserves, and a Gross Domestic Product with a steady rate of growth. It is clear that this growth will be translated into a demand for a greater importance in world relations, the first signs of which are already evident. Obviously, when the margins of further growth have been exhausted, China, like the other imperialist plunderers, will make use of force: plainly, today's growth carries within it tomorrow's *breakdown of order.*

But that growth is also creating the biggest proletarian army on earth, once more bringing to the fore the bourgeoisie-proletariat polarisation typical of capitalism: according to the *Boston Consulting Group*, in 2006 China surpassed France and Italy in the number of its (dollar) millionaires – 310,000 (compared with the 260,000 of 2005) as against the 265,000 in France and the 270,000 in Italy. Confronting those 50,000 additional millionaires, in the same period China's urban proletariat grew by almost 14 million.

And what goes for China goes for India. According to the United Nations Trade and Development Conference's *2007/2008 Report on the information technology economy*, China and India are playing an increasingly bigger role in information technology. In 1996, the most highly developed countries accounted for two-thirds of the sector's services and product exports, and the developing countries one-third. Today, the proportions are almost inverted (47 % and 53 %). If China is now the number one world exporter of technological products, India is in 8th place, but with a 37 % pace of growth between 2000 and 2005.

The city of Bangalore is the acknowledged symbol of this development. At the end of the 1980, the company Texas Instrument moved into the city, with a software development centre linked by satellite to Dallas. Other multinationals followed this example, 1992 saw the opening of the Software Technology Park, and Bangalore became India's capital of information technology. Today it has more than 1,200 companies, with over 250,000 employees specialising in the two main branches of information technology: 165,000 are engineers and software technicians, while 85,000 work in call centres, providing assistance all over the world.

With Lenin, we are aware that: « *It is not balance between powers that is impossible: capitalism (i.e. the nature of the power) makes balance impossible* ».

The new powers that today are sitting down at the table of the imperialist plunderers will soon be demanding a new partition, commensurate with their strength.

The greatest power in the world

For years, modish intellectuals have been talking about the disappearance of the working class, and about how the view of society as divided into classes is so dated. Restricting the analysis to the workers of the advanced metropolises, and muddling up income levels with social position, many thought to refute Marx by underlining how affluence was spreading and creating an extended « *middle class* ».

In fact, they were arguing with an imaginary Marx: the numbers of those who sell their labour in exchange for wages has continued to rise without interruption, even in the most developed countries.

Rather, it could be said that this world increase is precisely the clearest and most incontrovertible data of our age: according to the statistics of the *International Labour Organisation*, we can estimate that increase over ten years has been from 950 million wage-earners to one and a half billion – an increase of over 50 %.

Two specific points: the numbers employed in industry have increased at a faster than average rate: « *Behind these numbers we see millions of young Chinese, Indians, Indonesian, Vietnamese and Brazilian workers who from the turn of the century, have strengthened and will increasingly continue to strengthen our class* ».[92]

The other side of this increase is the fall in the number employed in agriculture: « *behind these figures we see thirty million people torn every year from the backwardness of the countryside, and slotted into the machine of modern capitalist production* ».[93]

These are the statistics of the numerical growth of the world's revolutionary forces: « *The bourgeoisie has not only forged the weapons that bring death to itself; it has also called into existence the men who are to wield these weapons – the modern working class – the proletarians (...) With the development of industry, the proletariat not only increases in number, it becomes concentrated in greater masses, its strength grows, and it feels that strength more (...) The workers begin to form combinations against the bourgeoisie, they club together in order to keep up the rate of wages (...) Here and there the contest breaks out into riots. Now and then the workers are victorious, but only for a time. The real fruit of their battle lies, not in the immediate result, but in the ever expanding union of the workers* ».[94]

The picture is well drawn in the *Manifesto*, although the workers Marx observed were only tens of thousands, and concentrated in a few countries. The numbers in today's game are very different, and the conditions more favourable – the concentration of workers in big firms, the educational level of the workforce, the opportunities for transport and communication.

« *The organisation of the proletarians into a class, and consequently into a political party, is continually being upset by the competition between the workers themselves. But it ever rises up again, stronger, firmer, mightier* ».[95]

The bourgeoisie incessantly attempts to divide the working class, employing every tool, including racism: but unity – i.e. ending competition between workers – is the only form of class defence, and because of this the inclination towards unity is strong.

There is certainly no hiding the difficulties inherent in *speaking* to these immense masses, divided by difference of language, culture and nationality: it is difficult, but possible, especially if operating in one of the main world powers, with a vast, well-educated proletariat, concentrated into large economic groups, with a low average age.

« *If we consider the present EU-27, we find before us a labour market of over 175 million wage earners, to whom a few million unregistered workers should be added. This is a young class, more than half below the age of forty, which boasts over 50 million workers, employees and skilled industrial workers in the strict sense of the term. It is a proletariat which is not uniformly distributed on the European market, but which is dislocated in a number of big urban and labour-market concentrations. International statistical analyses circulated in the last few months in the European Press among others, consider Paris and the Île-de-France, with over 1 million residents, and the great metropolitan centre of Milan, with a total of 7.4 million inhabitants, as the two leading metropolises in Europe* ».[96] Here is the most concentrated and most highly-qualified proletariat in the world: from here it is possible to begin to speak to the proletariat of the world about their struggle.

The bourgeoisie has had its day, and has produced its own *grave-diggers*. The testimonial of historical development must now be grasped by another class, a class: « *which is in itself the expression of the dissolution of all classes, nationalities, etc. within present society* ».

Chapter Four

The concrete task in a storm-tossed world

« *Confusion generates disorientation, but also a need for clarity, and it is the task of the Scientific Party to unwind the skein of social and political events. This is not so much a case of a process of internal assimilation within the consistent, organised minority. Rather, it is a bringing into our class, on the base of a solidly organised machine, Marxism as applied strategy and praxis alongside a determined political campaign: with a newspaper that over the years has acquired an unmistakably reputable, competent aspect and rock-solid authority among the masses: with the Party's books spreading its decades-old formulations, giving continuity and meaning to the transient memory of the working-class and focusing its attention on the forces and trends that matter, reaching far beyond the implacable immediacy and the fleeting triviality of everyday life* ».

Arrigo Cervetto, 1989

The world is changing quickly. It is difficult, today, for a young person to visualise the society in which he or she will live, work, and start a family in the years to come.

Today, history is again speeding up. As in the aftermath of the *first globalisation*: « *the shifts and changes that, based on the old criteria, would have taken centuries, are now completed in decades, even years. History has become rushed, much more rushed than our thoughts* » wrote Leon Trotsky.

The relative strength of the powers is changing at a great rate. During 2007, the economy of the USA grew by 1.9 %, and that of the EU by 2.7 %, but India's grew by 8.4 %, and China's by 10 %. Anyone can understand that such uneven growth creates very marked imbalances in the relative strength of the powers, and in their political weight in the field of global relations.

The differentials are likely to increase in the future. Economists make a variety of forecasts – influenced, obviously, by political considerations – as to when China's primacy as world power will be confirmed, but there is general agreement as to the extraordinary growth of China and India. One of the most authoritative forecasts, Angus Maddison's, estimates that in the period 2003/2030, China's share of the world GDP will grow from 14 % to 23.8 %, and India's from 5.61 % to 9.7 %, while that of the USA will decrease from 21 % to 18 %, Western Europe's from 19.46 % to 13.41 %, and Japan's from 6.68 % to 3.55 %.[100] The overall share lost by the USA, the EU and Japan will correspond approximately to that gained by China and India.

Until now, the development of the new powers has favoured the older countries: « *For a long time, it was the high development tempos of the new powers which permitted enduring paces in the metropolises. Not only: it was on those tempos that the old metropolises for decades based their reciprocal relations, balances, alliances – a balance of power in keeping with those relations of power*».[97]

Today the situation has changed: the dynamic that has permitted China to develop at a pace so far superior to that of the older countries has brought it to: « *a threshold of power which allows her to take part in the imperialist competition: she claims her place in the "new world order". This calls into question the consolidated equilibra between the old powers. This is obviously true not only for China – in a differentiated, uneven manner, it is true, for diverse emerging powers* ».

What does it mean when the emerging powers claim their place within the new world order, putting in question the established balances? « *The incessant movement which characterises imperialism bears within itself the seeds of catastrophe, of inevitable rupture in the world balance, of crises, of war* ».[98]

Common sense and *slothful thinking* repress this possibility: « *if there were no turbulent facts, the inertia of thought would be the best guarantee of order* » writes Trotsky. « *But turbulent facts have their own internal logic. Our slothful thought insists on not recognising them until the last minute ... Poor thought! It always ends up splattered against the wall of facts* ».[99]

Things happen even when one tries to *repress* their inevitability: things happen independently of one's *will*: « *Great events – the milestones that mark the turning points of history – are born when great causes intersect. And great causes, independently of our will, take shape in the course of our existence within society. Here lies their irresistible force (...) today, great and terrible events are resonating in the depths of all human "civilised" society. Those who attempt to seize their general nature and to call them by name, are branded visionaries by received wisdom* ».[100]

Six years after this was written, the First World War broke out, and *received wisdom was splattered against the wall of facts.*

Time is not so tight today: we still have some left. But how will we use this *time* that remains to us?

The imperialist powers are preparing for a clash, even those that present themselves in the guise of a peaceful power. This is because: « *the capitalists divide the world, not out of any particular malice, but because the degree of concentration which has been reached forces them to adopt this method in order to obtain profits. And they divide it "in proportion to capital" "in proportion to strength"* ».[101]

When Germany, on the rise at the end of an intense period of development that had allowed it to surpass the economic strength of Great Britain, found itself in possession of the same share of « *world economic territory* » as twenty years previously: « *what means other than war could there be under capitalism to overcome the disparity between the development of productive forces and the accumulation of capital on one side, and the division of colonies and spheres of influence on the other?* »[102]

Within the international debate there is a sharp awareness that the development of today's Germanys – China and India – will create the conditions for a future *breakdown of order.*

The Chinese economy's leap forward can be observed throughout the world. One significant example is that the biggest oil deal since the days of Saddam Hussein has been agreed between the new Iraq and the Chinese company CNPC: 3 billion dollars for a twenty-year exploitation of the al-Ahdab oilfield, capable of producing 90,000 barrels of crude per day.

Just as significant are Chinese investments in Africa, which have been described as a *Marshall Plan* (the programme of American investments that triggered economic recovery in western Europe at the end of the Second World War):« *(China) is building roads and railways, is exploiting oilfields, reserves of platinum, gold and other mineral resources. There has probably not been so much movement in Africa since the the 1950s* ».[103]

The West's hypocritical media stresses that China supplies arms to bloodthirsty regimes, that it has a pattern of « *crushing dissent* », is indifferent to trade union rights and has no respect for the environment, but also recognises that there can be no thought of putting a stop to business because « *China needs Africa's resources as much as Africa needs China's wealth* ».

It is a fact that China « *having achieved its imperialist maturity, is becoming an increasingly inconvenient world player, especially at the "African lottery" table. Only illusions packed tight with the ideologies of imperialism could have fuelled hopes of a Chinese dragon with "an enormous appetite but bad teeth"* ».[104]

What, though, will happen when competition becomes fiercer? Ian Buruma, New York university lecturer, considered to be one of the most knowledgeable experts on China, recalls Lenin's reference to Germany: « *no economy can keep up the same rate of growth indefinitely. Sooner or later there's a crisis (...) it's happened in the past. In some ways, the Germany of the 1900s, with its industrial strength, its educated but politically sterile middle class and its tendency towards aggressive nationalism, is very close to the Chinese template (...) China's aggressive nationalism could also prove lethal, if its economy were to stumble* ».[105] The academic's conclusion is not encouraging: « *this would serve no-one's interests, so we can only hope for the best* ».

The illusion that the end of the old bi-polar world divided by USA-USSR rivalry would open an era of peace has quickly evaporated before the reality of a multipolar world, in which big and median powers certainly do not exclude the use of arms from their conflicts.

It is understandable, therefore, that the political expert Nicolas Baverez observes in *Le point* that globalisation « *has not eradicated war, (...) economic crises, or revolutions* » and that « *war has returned to the fore in the lives and histories of the democracies, Europe included* ». He puts forward the theory that we *should not glorify war*, but neither should we deny it, and that we therefore need to provide ourselves with military means powerful enough to face a war, if necessary.

The imperialists *hope for the best*, but meanwhile they prepare for the inevitable. They prepare by investing enormous resources in arms and military research, by deploying the political and institutional tools that will make them strongest – as European imperialism is in the process of doing – and by spreading ideologies designed to justify and promote the massacre.

«Hearts and minds in America, Europe, Russia, Iraq, as in China, India, Japan or Brasil – everywhere - are nailed to the narrow world ideologies of each individual power's interests. They are nailed to Americanism, which proclaims that the USA *is the universal shining light of freedom and progress, but which seeks in war a palliative for its decline: to Europeanism, which boasts Europe as a power for peace, but arms it for its future wars: to the inept and corrupt nationalism of the Arab bourgeoisie, which uses religious fanaticism and terrorism to ward off a bankruptcy nurtured by rivers of oil and a century of intrigues with imperialism: to new nationalisms – Hindu, Mandarin or Brazilian – which fashion new monsters for new conflicts out of old ideologies».*[106]

These ideologies are primarily for internal consumption: the powers haven't much need to justify themselves externally, but they do need to tie their own proletariat, and their young, to their chariot. The interests of imperialism are the interests of the few, but around these interests the powers have to mobilise the consensus of the masses.

In short, throughout the world *there is still time*, and the bourgeoisie are using it to prepare themselves for the natural *epilogue* of capitalist development. The proletariat must also prepare.

In order to do this, it requires above all the science of Marxism, because ignorance has generated rebellions, but never revolution. It must develop its revolutionary organisation, because spontaneity and agitations can produce myths and heroes, but are not enough for victory. It will have to swim against the current of *received wisdom*, of *slothful thought*, fighting imperialist ideology in whatever form it presents itself, starting with that which attacks our own youth and workers.

We have to understand how imperialism prepares itself, what are the potential revolutionary energies, how we can bring consciousness and organisation to such impressive forces: what it means to be a Bolshevik today.

Today, our society can offer the young only illusions: the battle for Communism is something concrete, tangible.

«*For the first time in hundreds and thousands of years, the promise to "reply" to war between the slave-owners by a revolutions of the slaves directed against* all *slave-owners has been completely fulfilled, and is being fulfilled, despite all difficulties*» wrote Lenin in 1921. «*We have made the start. When, at what date and time and the proletarians of which nation will complete this process, is not important. The important thing is that the ice has been broken, the road is open, the way has been shown*».[107]

We believe that to take this road, in this tortured age of ours, is the best way to give meaning to life.

Changing the future

The forecast is for storms

Hans Magnus Enzensberger reports a dialogue between Marx and a British baronet on the issue of military spending: « *I objected: "But suppose those who govern Europe agreed to limit armaments, a thing that could significantly reduce the burden that weighs on the people: what, then, would become of the revolution that according to you will inevitably break out?"*

"Ah" – was the reply – "they can't do it. All sorts of fears and suspicions will make such an agreement impossible. In fact, as science progresses, the burden will become ever heavier, since perfection of the means of destruction will keep pace: every year increasing sums will have to be earmarked for costly war machinery. It's a vicious circle, there is no way out" ».[108]

The issue hasn't moved on much since then. Today there are still naive pacifists deluding themselves that they can influence governments, pushing them to limit military spending, but reality consistently demonstrates that Marx was right. In the course of 2007, world military spending has returned to Cold War levels, reaching the astronomical figure of 1,200 billion dollars: the imperialists are all arming, starting with the USA, where 50 % of world military spending is concentrated. For American imperialism, this is 4.7 % of their GDP, much of it invested in « *research and development* » involving new weapons: airborne laser to destroy enemy jets, microwave-powered weapons, electromagnetic rays, high-frequency weapons capable of evaporating whatever they strike.

The country of *harmonious growth* is also arming: in 2007 came China's sensational destruction of an obsolete weather satellite, using laser rays. This was prominently featured in the media, which underlined that Peking *should not have had* the technology: the process (its Chinese name is «*strike to kill*», just so as not to leave any doubts about its final intent) demonstrated that the Chinese military were now able to strike objects moving at a speed of over 7 kilometres per second, and was a clear signal to whoever believed they could use long-range missiles to strike with impunity at Chinese installations.

Defensive aims also underlie the construction of the first Chinese fleet of aircraft carriers, whose *mission* is to guarantee safe passage on sea routes essential for transportation of raw materials and fuel. The ships are to be protected by the new *invisible* Song submarines like the one which, in the summer of 2008, tracked an American aircraft carrier over a lengthy period, and was only spotted when it surfaced.

The same goes for aerospace research: « *With the launch of the "Divine Vessel", Peking has crossed the threshold of human flight in space, the third power in history to take this step. In China's deliberately flaunted parade of economic, military and strategic power, these space vehicles are primarily one-way political missiles, pointed towards every association of forces in the world balance. What sort of relationship are they preparing with America, with Europe, Russia, India, Japan? The rebus of the new and intangible events let loose by Chinese imperialism will be solved by the new circumstances of the global balance. A competition involving such a clash of giants will dismantle the illusion that we can endlessly walk "the razor's edge" of political balance, if this is all that separates imperialism's peace from war* ».[109]

This launch was followed by another, on 25th September 2008, involving three astronauts.

An impressive amount of resources have been deployed: many commentators agree that figures released by China's Defence Department underplay the cost: China, whose Defence Department budget increases by 20 % every year, probably does not want to alarm the international community.

The other big Asian power, India, has been buying arms worth 45 billion dollars on the American market for the last five years, after having for decades employed second-hand Soviet weapons. The land of Ghandian non-violence launched its first nuclear missile from an undersea base in 2008. And like all the other emerging powers, India is increasing its military spending at a pace superior to the growth of its GDP, while its goal of bringing its navy up to a strength equal to that of Britain has already been realised.

Even Russia is re-arming: wishing to again play the role of a great power, it is experimenting with thermobaric weapons, a mix of explosives and fuel made by nuclear manipulation of these materials: « *invisible* » planes: new generation missiles and submarines.

And the *enemy in our own house* has been no less busy. European imperialism allocates 1.2 % of its GDP to military spending, but increasingly there are calls for more.

In fact, the process of European unification has posed fresh problems for the defence sector. On the one hand, the fall of internal barriers has made redundant many of the troops deployed to guard frontiers, the first effect of which has been the end of compulsory military service, since the current requirement is for a more *professional* corps capable of carrying out missions abroad. On the other hand, the need for greater autonomy from the USA in the event of a conflict drives the EU to provide itself with independent military systems. This is the case with the satellite network which will make up the *future constellation* of the European satellite system *Galileo*, the direct competitor of the American *GPS* (supposedly *Galileo* can identify a ground target six times more precisely than *GPS*).

It is well-known that the GPS system was fundamental for the USA in directing their *intelligent bombs* in Serbia in 1999 and in the Afghanistan wars, this being the reason for the attachment of European military lobbies to the *Galileo* project.

Officially *Galileo*, which will be operational from 2013, is for civilian use, in spite of the fact that all warships currently being built in Europe will be capable of communicating with and using the system. In any case, the dual nature of all these programmes – civil and military – is widely known.

What is the point of producing such mountains of weapons?

In an interview with *Handelsblatt* on 3rd September 2008, Volker Perthes, the director of *Stiftung fur Wissenschaftspolitik* stated that: « *New big powers are threatening the balance, the risks of war are increasing (...) the world presents as more and more unsafe and complex* ».

A recently published essay collection, co-ordinated by Jean-Hervé Lorenzi of the Edmond de Rothschild Finance Company, carries an extremely expressive title, *The capitalist war will take place* : « *The collective hopes of the planet fantasise a harmonious alignment towards a world in which peoples and individuals will be able to share out world resources in the most efficient and equitable way possible. This hope (...) conceals tensions that already exist and that will grow stronger in the years to come among the big emerging powers and those who have been the "privileged" of history* ».

This is the point of the mountains of weapons produced in the world: to fight the next *capitalist war*, when, with pacifist illusions defeated, it *will take place.*

The enemy is in our own house

On the subject of war, Leon Trotsky wrote: « *Suddenly, war shows us that we are still moving on all fours, and that we have not yet emerged from the womb of our history's age of barbarism* ».[110]

The ruling class has to deny this reality: it has to justify its atrocities, veiling them with noble ideals: it has to convince young people that it is a worthwhile thing to die defending its interests. Not an easy task, which is why an impressive ideology-producing machine works away to make sure that *the ideas of the ruling class are the ruling ideas.*

«*Every era has its false consciousness, its variant of bourgeois ideology in which the ideas of the ruling class become the common perception. Yesterday's world was reflected in the ideologies of the division into two opposing sides headed by the USA and the USSR. It was the world of the Cold War, of the balance of terror, of the myths of Western democracy countered by those of false socialism. Today's ideology is the union of the world in a big global market, where great and very great powers have learnt the good manners of peaceful competition. China is staging its "peaceful rise" to power. Europe claims to be a benign power, because it has superseded its nation-states born of blood and iron. America sees itself as a model and guardian of that single world, welded together by freedom of industry, trade and commerce*».[111]

It is always easier to grasp the mystification of someone else's *false consciousness*, as is the case with American imperialism. On 1st May 2003, President Bush hailed «*victory*» in Iraq against Saddam Hussein by jumping from a military jet onto the deck of the aircraft carrier Lincoln, in aircrew dress and with a flying helmet under his arm: he placed himself in front of a banner that read: «*mission accomplished*» and declared: «*We fought for freedom and peace in the world: thanks to you the tyrant has fallen and Iraq is free*».

The hundreds of thousands of innocent Iraqi victims, almost all fallen *after* the end of the war, the terrorists who carry out attacks on a daily basis, the dead and mutilated Americans, are mostly young people from the poorest areas, and immigrants enlisting for the promise of citizenship: it is difficult to say that there has been an increase in *freedom and peace in the world.* From Europe, it is easy to see how ideology distorts the truth.

This also concerns the emerging powers. It is the case in China, where young nationalists counter-demonstrated against the anti-Chinese protests linked to events in Tibet.

According to Minxin Pei – director of the *China Program* at *Washington's Carnegie Endowment for International Peace*, these were not organised by the regime, but were spontaneous, like the demonstrations in May 2005 against

Japan, which was requesting a permanent place on the *UN Security Council*, and those of April 1999, when the American embassy was attacked after the Chinese embassy in Belgrade was bombed by mistake.

Unlike the anti-totalitarian students of *Tienanmen Square*, these young people have grown up during the years of economic and political progress in China, which they see as a country that « *offers individual freedom and has created great opportunities* ». Grafted onto traditional suspicions against the West, this has given birth to a new type of nationalist mix. It is an apparently paradoxical case of economic globalisation developing nationalist feeling among the young.

« *The* International Herald Tribune *carries a headline "China's loyal youth". It goes on to explain that it is naive to think that Chinese youth opposes its government because it is repressive and run by old men. The young "belong to the Han ethnic group, and are patriotic". Chinese graduates are optimistic: they believe they will soon own houses and cars. Only when they start working will they see the disasters caused by corruption and bureaucratic inefficiency, and then they will become critical. Aurore Merle and Michael Sztanke, in their study "Chinese students: Who are the élites of tomorrow?" published in 2006, argued that university students are unanimous in their dream of a "strong China" on the international scene* ».[112]

On the other hand: « *It would not be surprising if Chinese youth and intellectuals turned out to be in the front line of the illusion that they can restore the Middle Empire to its former splendour. They no longer see themselves as a civilisation surrounded by barbarians, but may want to believe they are part of an empire restored to glory among other empires, an imperialism among imperialisms. In its history, the proletariat has experienced nationalism in all its guises, including "rabid nationalism". It would be hard for anything, whether original or counterfeit, whether arriving from China or from the other countries of immense Asia, to surprise us. One thing is certain: an immense proletariat is accumulating in those endless metropolises, and its political and economic situation will find no solutions, but only illusions, in the ideologies spawned by its ruling class* ».[113]

It is easy for us to understand the reasoning behind Chinese nationalist ideology and to see the true interests it conceals: it is much more difficult to oppose the ideological productions of our own in-house imperialism.

We have already recalled that the declaration signed at the end of the fiftieth anniversary celebrations for the *Treaty of Rome*, seen as the founding act of the European Union, clearly indicated the self-image the EU wished to project, with its statement that *European unification shows that we have learnt the lessons of a history marked by bloody conflict.*

We are full in the midst of the benevolent Europe ideology: a Europe that has overcome internal disagreements and that for this very reason can present itself to the world as the voice of peace and well-being: « *We commit ourselves to finding peaceful solutions to world conflict, in order that human beings do not fall victim to wars, terrorism and violence. The European Union wishes to promote freedom and development in the world (...) The European Union will continue to promote democracy, stability and well-being even beyond its borders* ».

From its first beginnings, Marxism has identified the imperialist context of this tendency towards unification. The struggle against imperialism and social-imperialism has been written into our elaborations for decades.

Clarity about the goal of European union – the requirement for Europe to be able to compete with powers of continental dimensions – allows us to understand that rejection of the old nationalisms has served only to forge a new nationalism that will function better in tomorrow's clashes.

« *The illusion just celebrated in Berlin to mark the fiftieth anniversary of the treaties that founded the EU is that the unity of Europe means peace, since it has confederated the powers that had been at each others' throats in two world wars. It is really true that the best lies are half-truths. Banishing war from the Rhine or from the English Channel does not mean peace: it means coalescing the weapons of the Old Continent in order to send them elsewhere: in fact, European peace coexists with war in Afghanistan or in Iraq, and today's peacekeeping missions are training the forces for the wars of tomorrow* ».[114]

The first task of European internationalists must be the struggle against the ideologies of their own imperialism - to denounce its interests and to put up an intransigent opposition to nationalism and racism.

« *The fate of the proletariat in Europe has been to experience on its own back all the various types of nationalisms, up to the imperialist Europeanism of our day. From this point of view, the nationalism of the Middle Empire has very little to add to the school of imperialist democracy. The ideologies of imperialism are born, die, are resurrected, and move between the continents of the globe on the backs of the exploited class. "We have no country" the internationalists proclaimed in 1918. They left us the legacy of knowing that internationalism is not only the ideal of the emancipation of humanity: it is a practical necessity* ».[115]

Ideologies of decay and passivity

Marxism opposes a scientific view of reality to ideology, which is: « *a "false consciousness" a view of reality turned upside down and inside out. A theoretical position which in fact essentially falsifies the truth and which, behind an outwardly neutral and universal vision of the world, hides the defence and justification of one specific point of view. It is the widespread and continual attempt of whichever social class is dominant in any particular era to pass off its own peculiar interests and values as common to all* ».[116]

The ruling class actually goes further, even providing its own opposition ideologies. Aspects of capitalism that are open to criticism are separated from any social analysis and flagged up as weapons in the clashes between big business groups and fractions of the bourgeoisie.

A typical example is the ecologist current – within which it is no coincidence that the Catholic Church itself has taken up position – which tends to restrict criticism of capitalism to its destructive attitude towards the environment.

The subject is not new: Engels had stressed that capitalist behaviour towards Nature attempts to control it while ignoring its laws. Communism is the true environmentalist, because it goes to the roots of the problem – the mode of production: « *If we limit ourselves to observing how capitalist development ransacks the Earth, we will not understand the reality of the situation. To imagine a capitalist development that would respect Nature is to delude ourselves and others: to become, in effect, apologists for capitalism as it now is. Working to organise and raise the consciousness of the "historic driving force" of society is the only way of returning to an organic interchange between man and Nature, no longer spontaneous, but on a scientific base. This means freeing the power of science, and the technology born out of large-scale industry, from the chains of the bourgeois mode of production* ».[117]

It is no surprise that yesterday's anti-nuclear protesters, having discovered that they had simply advanced the interests of the petroleum multinationals, moved on to support the bio-fuels that have subsequently been implicated in the cereal prices explosion, and are now champions of nuclear power – all the while convinced that they are independent spirits opposing economic power, while in reality they have been supporting specific interests.

Then there is the *NIMBY (not in my back-yard)* attitude – I can't change the world, but I can at least make sure that the negative aspects of this society stay far away from *my garden*.

Egoism and individualism are liberally promoted, and the message is hammered home: your life may be unsatisfactory, but you can change it by «*playing the lead role*»: a self-made individual on your way up the social ladder.

In this scenario there is no prospect of collective emancipation, only the sad hope of being able to sell oneself at a good price, the hope of becoming part of the class that rules with money, while even *rights* become merely a statement of one's personal individualism.

Today the form in which these rights are expressed is particularly degrading, going so far as to claim the right to use drugs, in other words, to damage the organ that has allowed us to become the dominant species of the planet. That certain behaviour – use of recreational drugs, alcohol abuse – has spread among young people does not reduce its dangers, or justify it.

We have always opposed the use of recreational drugs, even at the time of theories about *right-wing individualist* drugs, like heroin, and *social left-wing* drugs, such as cannabis. We are even more so now that scientific research has evidenced the dangers of even the so-called mild drugs. There was a sensation when in 2007 the British daily the *Independent*, after having been a champion of the campaign to liberalise the use of mild drugs, publicly recanted and apologised with a front page headlined « *Cannabis: an apology* ». It had discovered that even as its previous campaign had been obtaining the desired results, the number of cannabis addicts had gone through

To restore the weak and serve the strong

When the bourgeoisie achieved the position of ruling class, it became reactionary: at that point, its goal was the preservation of its power and the justification of its status quo.
The bourgeoisie of imperialism's time of decay no longer needed to develop the social sciences. An important step for the bourgeoisie's search for ideologies was when it "naturally" turned to the oldest and most widely-tested conservative ideology, religion, and its organisation, the Church.
For 2000 years, the Church has preached social order and justified its class divisions, from the writing of Saint Paul's Letters: « *Obey the rulers who have authority over you. Only God can give authority to anyone, and He puts these rulers in their places of power. Those who oppose the authorities are opposing what God has done* ». (Letter to the Romans). And: « *All are to remain in the station to which they have been called. Have you been called to be a slave? Do not worry* ». (First Letter to the Corinthians).
Here, obviously, are the origins of *Rerum novarum,* considered to be the current basis of the social doctrines of the Church, which says that « *to remove social inequalities from the world is impossible* » and that « *to suffer and to endure is the heritage of the human race* ».

the roof, going so far as to cause – according to the *London Institute of Psychiatry* – a 10 % increase in mental health problems among British youth.

Moreover, both prohibition and legalisation are based on the illusion that in the capitalist market legal instruments can be used to eliminate trade in a commodity that guarantees extremely high profit levels. For his part, Marx put it well in *Book 1* of *Capital*: « *With adequate profit, capital is very bold. A certain ten percent will ensure its employment anywhere; twenty percent certain will produce eagerness; fifty percent positive audacity; a hundred percent will make it ready to trample on all human laws; three hundred percent and there is not a crime at which it will scruple, nor a risk it will not run, even to the chance of its owner being hanged* ».

In the fight against drug use, too, the defeat of capitalist profit is the only way of resolving the problem.

For Marx, religion: « *is the sigh of the oppressed creature* » and in this sense is « *the opium of the people* », that it mitigates – if only with imaginary consolations – the suffering arising from class oppression. To fight against religion in a class-divided society is almost like refusing pain-killing drugs to a sick person: the struggle is with the disease: once this is defeated, the human race will have no more need for pain-killing drugs.

« *Marxists have always confronted the question of religion very seriously, despite their firm opposition, as dialectical materialists and hence atheists, to all religions and all Churches, which today are inevitably the tools of bourgeois reaction. In an article of 1909, Lenin returned to the question, recalling Engels' repeated condemnation of those who wished to insert atheism – as a declaration of war on religion – into the programme of the workers' party, observing, among other things, how this was the way « to revive interest in religion and to prevent it from really dying out* ».[118]

For Marx, people make religion, not the other way round. « *Religious suffering is at one and the same time the expression of real suffering and a protest against real suffering. Religion is the sigh of the oppressed creature, the heart of a heartless world, and the soul of soulless conditions* ».[119]

For this reason, a consistent atheist cannot downgrade the issue to one of personal choice, but must struggle to « *abandon illusion* » and in order to go beyond a social situation that needs illusions, must fight for Communism.

It is useful to also underline that those who propose to change the world require all the lucidity, the strength and the intelligence that Nature has granted them.

In addition, the issue of rights has long been clear: « *in the age of imperialism, Engels' teaching on the historical right is of particular relevance, both because the so-called "rights" are produced on a daily basis, and because they are presented in all kinds of ways (...) in order to avoid every possible misunderstanding concerning parliamentary tactics and the historical tasks of the revolutionary proletariat, Engels makes it clear that: "The right to a revolution is the only real "historical right"* ».[120]

For this *true right* we are quite disposed to leave to the ruling class all the poisoned fruits of its fake rights and its illusions.

A world in conflict

The magnificent process of proletarianization that is taking place in the world is throwing millions of people into the vortex of class war: « *those same millions, snatched from the frozen underdevelopment of a peasant lifestyle, are daily being added to our class, to the ranks of the international proletariat. New names appear in the pages of working-class struggle, in China, in Eastern Europe, along the Mediterranean or in the metropolises of Latin America* ».[121]

This is a logical process: « *Strikes are a "natural economic phenomenon" and therefore should be studied as part of nature, as part of capitalist society's nature* » wrote Arrigo Cervetto in *Class Struggles and the Revolutionary Party*.

The news from China tells how the proletariat in that country are involved in tough opposition to capitalist exploitation, and how a new generation of working-class militants are appearing on the scene of class struggle. Statistics on strikes – which are illegal, as are independent trade union organisations – are provided by the police force and are certainly under-estimates, but clearly indicate how the year by year trend is steadily upwards.

« *One concise fact about the struggle: if it is true that the Chinese economy, in its headlong development, has marched ahead for years, at what economists call « double-digit growth" rates, i.e. of at least 10 % per year, labour disputes have also increased at double-digit rates, but at a much higher level than the growth of the economy. For example, in 2005 there were almost one thousand disputes per day, a 20 % increase with respect to 2004. (...) It is not a sudden increase: labour disputes, no matter how much they are constricted and limited by objective conditions, by the youthfulness of the labour force, by the various forms of state apparatus repression, by the Party's mediation and by the lack of an effective trade union to organise them, have matured, grown, and become measurable by now over a sufficient period of years, to be analysed in some detail*».[122]

Thanks to this dynamic by which strikes have increased tenfold in 12 years, a start has been made on wresting some concessions from the ruling class. From 1st January 2008, a new law based on German and British regulations gives employees some limited protection, though it remains largely unapplied even in large centres or work such as Shenzen.

From the same Chinese experience emerges the indispensable nature of worker unity, in the face of widely diverging treatment for identical work. The average annual wage in cities like Peking and Shanghai is 3,650 euros, but the average for the whole of China is 2,275: while the phenomenon of delocalisation, well-known to western workers, is spreading, with the transfer of significant levels of production to places where wages are much lower, such as Vietnam.

But struggles are not only taking place in China. Wherever the proletariat exists, the classic form of struggle reappears: this is the case for construction workers in Dubai, who in one of the richest countries in the world earn between 2.75 and 7 dollars per day. It is the case for the employees of *Ford* in St. Petersburg, who demanded pay rises of between 580 and 780 euro, in the face of inflation running at over 9 %: for the 20,000 Vietnamese workers who brought to a halt one of *Nike's* biggest factories in protest against a monthly wage of 40 euro before tax, which was not enough for them to live on in view of the current rise in the price of food: and at *Renault's Dacia* factory in Pitesti, Romania, where 14,000 workers – after downing tools for 3 weeks – won a substantial wage rise.

We have already frequently described the same situation: «*Millions of new proletarians are joining the ranks of our class. We have estimated that in the next few years the annual increment will be equal to one half of the waged workers of Italy. Inevitably, this enormous process of proletarianization will bring contradictions and new class struggles. These struggles will throw up a vanguard who will be forced by objective circumstances to reflect upon their situation and experiences*».[123]

But workers' struggles go on in the older metropolises, too: «*In a phase of profound and prolonged social passivity, there is no problem about a breakdown in social order. "Specific" struggles, no matter how fierce, cannot lead to changes in the cycle: indeed, their very nature means that they are rarely severe, and always last only a short time. This does not mean that a phase of social passivity is without contradictions*».[124]

In fact, the main new development has taken place in Europe: «*the imperialist struggle itself has imposed on Europe a labour-force market on a continental scale, so much so that the "European worker" Arrigo Cervetto glimpsed when the European Common Market was set up has now become about two hundred million wage earners. This is an unprecedented fact in the "forces of class relationships" in Europe and the rest of the world, and would be an objective advantage in the unprecedented nature of the new strategic phase*».[125]

It is one more facet of globalisation that it brings together workers who live in very different national conditions: today the need for international solidarity, and the requirement to link up struggles that cross over national boundaries, is no longer to be found only in the pages of the *Manifesto*, but is increasingly a concrete fact of life for *one and a half billion* workers.

« *The Russian proletarian masses have drawn from the Bolshevik Party an unequalled degree of consciousness "of what must be done" and they have won. The same has not happened in Western Europe, and the international proletariat have paid the price in a very heavy defeat* ».[126] The 1900s was the century that displayed the superior nature of the Bolshevik model, the model that our scientific formulation has synthesised into the Science-Party.

Therefore: « *The end of the Bolshevik Party – part of a world-wide backlash – in no way reduces that party's importance in the history of the world. At the time of its revolutionary rise, when it represented the true proletarian vanguard, it was the most honest party in history (...) it told the workers the truth, the whole truth and nothing but the truth. Due to this fact alone, it conquered their trust like no other party in the world* ».[127]

Marxist science allows us to understand the world in which we live, to analyse its crises, to see the possible outcome of its development, but the revolutionary party, speaking only the truth, is what must turn theory into political struggle.

To do so, this party must be organised: it must have newspapers and publications that state its positions, must be self-financing to be truly independent, and it must be present among young people and workers, through a network of volunteers and activists. When the Leninist current started up after the war it modelled itself on the Bolshevik Party, building a network of workers' groups around the paper *Lotta Comunista.*

As had happened in Lenin's party, circulating the newspaper was an education in organisation: it imposed a consistent activity, pushing the activists towards daily contact with real live workers. It also made possible the creation of a network of consistent supporters, a sphere of influence for revolutionary positions: it allowed militants to take on responsibilities at various levels, and organised meetings for the spread and deeper understanding of propaganda. It created a political life independent of the bourgeoisie and the bourgeoisie's electoral rituals, newspapers and campaigns.

It is natural that bourgeois intellectuals should attack this model. Attacks and accusations against the Bolshevik party model will last as long as the age of imperialism. The ruling classes will never cease to batter away at the shape and the experiences of the party, for the simple reason that it brings the proletariat to the threshold of its own world party, and international revolution.

« *The arguments are boringly repetitive: that there is no freedom of criticism, no democracy, that there is control from the top, sectarianism, etc. We recall that such arguments have followed hard upon each others' heels for the whole of the last century, and are now cropping up again. Often it has been, and continues to be, a case of academic debates among "professors", or even worse, among supposed generals without an army, whose discussions are void, since the consequences of their discussions are nil* ».[128]

What features is it essential for the party to have? According to Lenin: « *in the first place, "one of the fundamental conditions for a Bolshevik victory" is "absolute centralisation and the tightest working-class discipline". On this last, he asks: "How is discipline in the proletariat's revolutionary party maintained?"* »

He provides three indicators: the most absolute dedication to the cause, organisation and a capacity to "blend" with the masses, and thirdly, correct strategy and tactics. Without these three conditions, Lenin observes, attempts to create discipline will turn "into soap bubbles, empty phrases, farce".

« *On the shape of the party, Lenin provides the International with the following synthesis: dedication to the cause and organised work among the masses, fused to white heat by scientific formulation. And here, in the light of the experiences of October, the detailed features of a party able for the age of imperialism begin to emerge: this is what we mean by "the Bolshevik model of the party"* ».[129]

From this point, from taking up the Bolshevik model again, begins the building of the revolutionary party in Italy in the post-war period.

«*A party that demands a long course of theoretical and practical education, and an acquisition of consciousness and knowledge that will require time, great commitment and dedication. It is a party model which by continual training of its militants, by providing them with all the necessary tools, is the complete negation of that dependence on blind faith, on constraint, on administration and grey bureaucracy that characterised that tragic parody, Stalinism.*

In truth, the Bolshevik party represented the highest historical level of raised consciousness within the real Communist movement. It represented, and continues to represent, a choice for freedom and inevitably of struggle against "the way things are". A struggle carried forward by collective work that allows the limits of a petty and misleading individualism, of the cult of personality, to be overcome. Overcome, precisely within the context of that "tightest and iron-hard discipline" which is not imposed, but is a choice made freely and with full understanding».[130]

The Bolshevik party is a party for the young generations: «*The youth of the revolutionary generation coincided with that of the working-class movement*» wrote Trotsky. «*It was the era of the 18 to 30 year-olds. The older revolutionaries could be counted on the fingers of one hand, and seemed old. The movement had no concept of careerism, it lived within its faith in the future, within its own spirit of sacrifice. There was neither routine nor formal convention, no theatrical gestures or striking of rhetorical attitudes*».[131]

Today we are once again living in the era of the *18 to 30 year-olds*, young men and women who will live through the epilogue to the *second globalisation*: today's actions are creating the conditions for the conflicts of a not too distant future.

«*There is a maxim of Trotsky's that we have often had occasion to recall in the course of the years. "Neither laugh nor weep". Which means, don't be knocked flat by difficulties, but don't glory in a moment of success. Every situation, whether negative or positive, contains margins for some future outcome (...) The outcomes and the margins of revolutionary activity should always be analysed in the light of a firm strategic perspective. For us today, it is to work at the fresh task of establishing a party on the Bolshevik model within the metropolises of European imperialism*».[132]

This is the goal before us: « *This perspective cannot but be the establishment of the party, our party on the Bolshevik model, in the European metropolises. Which means to work so that within one generation – the deadline for China's full imperialist maturity – the Leninist party will be rooted in one of the warring continental powers. A party formed in struggle with its own imperialism, a science-party whose formulations can relate, on the level of consciousness, to whatever situation the inevitable struggles of the young Asian proletariat will bring about* ».[133]

The Communist Choice

« *One cannot give the order to advance without having studied in detail every form that the struggle can take, without following its every stage while it moves from one form to another, so that one is able to define the situation from one moment to the next, without losing sight of the overall nature of the struggle and its ultimate aim: the complete and definitive abolition of all exploitation and all oppression* ».

Lenin, 1894

In conclusion: the changes we are seeing are the end of an era. For the first time, the new states appearing on the world scene possess populations superior in number to the populations of all the current big powers put together (China –1,300 million, India – about one billion, compared with the USA – 300 million, Europe – 480 million, and Japan –130 million). In addition, although it is not unknown for a capitalist country to have a high rate of growth, it has never before been the case that this rate has reached 10 % per year, over a number of consecutive years. The way China has burst onto the world market: the struggle of the old powers to resist their relative decline, from the Iraq war for the USA to unification for Europe: successive crises on a number of levels, from the subprime crisis to the price of oil, from the price of food to a financial crisis of dimensions unknown since the end of the Second World War: every day news turns into history in front of our very eyes.

Today Marx's scientific prophecy about the development of Asia and the shift of the world's centre of gravity towards the Pacific basin is being fully realised: an upheaval that can be likened to the end of an era in the 1500s, when the discovery of America led to the decline of the Mediterranean and the shift of trade and shipping to the Atlantic. That shift marked a vital stage in the struggle of the bourgeoisie to assert itself as the ruling class.

In his *Dialectics of Nature*, Engels writes about the 1500s, the end of one era: « *It was the greatest progressive revolution that mankind has so far experienced, a time which called for giants and produced giants: giants in power of thought, passion and character, in universality and learning. The men who founded the modern rule of the bourgeoisie had anything but bourgeois limitations. On the contrary, the adventurous character of the time inspired them to a greater or lesser degree. There was hardly any man of importance then living who had not travelled extensively, who did not command four or five languages, who did not shine in a number of fields*».[134]

The world of today, with its enormous contradictions, needs its version of the *men of the 1500s*, ready to confront the times that are to come. In our metropolises, amid the depths of self-centred affluence, behind the second-rate lifestyles of a decadent society, are remarkable young men and women who will soon take up the task of defeating the ruling class.

Today even bourgeois economists acknowledge that Marxism has the most efficient theoretical tools for interpreting the contemporary world: «*If one wants to analyse today's world market capitalism, the important section of the intellectual "toolbox" lies in what Marx and some of his followers wrote*» declares Pascal Lamy, director of the World Trade Organisation. «*Globalisation itself is only a stage in the history of market capitalism, just as Marx thought*».

Today, the revolution has immense forces available to it: «*first serfs freed from the land, then assistants in craft workshops, later manufacturing workers in factories, finally proletarians of the modern age, concentrated in the great industries. A young class, for long forced by history to fight alongside and under the bourgeoisie against the remains of the former society*».[135]

Today, that proletariat has grown to almost one and a half billion, and every day sees its numbers increase: their vanguard is concentrated in the big economic conglomerations, their average age is low, and they have all had a basic education. That proletariat is now capable of pursuing its own independent struggle against a social system which has become a brake on human progress itself.

The ruling class may repeat endlessly that Communism is Utopianism, that the notion of a society in which production is at the service of the whole of humanity and not just of a few is an illusion: to think that our current mode of production is eternal, and that the human race can never know other and more advanced forms of social organisation – *this* is Utopianism, and illusion.

There is a need for young people who want to commit themselves to this goal, who are capable of rejecting the individualism and passivity that distinguishes bourgeois morality, in order to embrace a higher morality, higher values.

Lenin asked: « *But is there such a thing a communist ethics? Is there such a thing as communist morality? Of course there is. It is often suggested that we have no ethics of our own: very often the bourgeoisie accuse us Communists of rejecting all morality (...) We reject the morality invoked by the bourgeoisie, who based ethics on God's commandments (...) or (...) on idealist or semi-idealist phrases which always amounted to something very similar to God's commandments. We reject any morality based on extra-human and extra-class concepts. We say that they are deceptions, dupery* ».[136]

And he goes on to say that capitalist society is founded: « *on the principle: rob or be robbed: work for others or make others work for you: be a slave-owner or be a slave* ».

Communist morality is neither the slave-owner morality, nor the morality of a slave. It lies, Lenin tells us, in the struggle against exploitation and egoism: « *against the psychology and the habit which says: I seek my own profit, and don't care a rap for anything else... When people tell us about morality, we say: to a Communist, all morality lies in this united discipline and in conscious mass struggle against the exploiters!* »

The machinery for this *conscious mass struggle* exists. It *exists* in an organisation modelled on the Bolshevik Party, which has newspapers and publications, premises and militants, which is present in workplaces and among the youth. There *is* a party which has no truck with bourgeois careerism and personal interest, in which there is a *united and solid communist discipline.*

It has been no easy matter to get as far as this: to take back the tools of Marxist science: to join anew the threads that the counter-revolution had snapped: to meet democrats and fascists, liberals and stalinists head-on.

But this party is alive again, right in the middle of a Europe that saw the birth of the working-class movement, and which today is one of the main imperialist powers on the world scene, which has a large, youthful and concentrated proletariat. The gamble is to strengthen the revolutionary party to the point where it can act as a compass for the masses when class conflict turns bitter and opens up for the oppressed a new *assault on Heaven.*

In Europe, and in its strongholds of waged labour, the decisive battles of a new era will be fought tomorrow: and from here we can speak to the great masses of Asia, using the universal language of *working-class internationalism.*

For this, we have to: « *work in depth among the masses, to prepare and organise the vanguard of our class, to allow it, when the contradictions of imperialism bring about world catastrophe, to lead the masses towards the only way out: proletarian revolution. We are revolutionaries because we know that the choice the future holds for the human race is between a revolution for a classless society and a new imperialist war, a war which would perpetuate "the state of things as they are", as has happened in the past.* »[137]

Here is the task for those young people who want to play a part in our age, who are capable of raising their eyes from the material and moral poverty of our times, who can continue the struggle fought by generations of revolutionaries before them.

The imperialist world is becoming unceasingly more complex. Its contradictions are becoming increasingly sharper. Already the thunder of a revolutionary period can be heard, and revolutionary certainties are becoming stronger: « *Victory will be on the side of the exploited, for on their side is life, numerical strength, the strength of the mass, the strength of all the inexhaustible sources of all that is selfless, dedicated and honest, all that is surging forward and awakening to the building of the new (...) Victory will be theirs* ».[138]

Notes

women must work together

[1] Renato Pastorino, "Giovani e salariati nello scorrimento sociale (*Youth and wage-earners in a changing society*)". In: *Il Compito Inedito (The unprecedented Task*), Lotta Comunista Editions, 2006.
[2] Friedrich Engels, *Critique of the Erfurt Programme*, 1891.
[3] Faared Zakaria, *The future of American power*. In: *Foreign Affairs*, May-June 2008.
[4] Leon Trotsky, *Their Morals and Ours*, "Dialectic Interdependence of End and Means". First published in New International, Vol. IV No. 6, June 1938.
[5] Lenin, *The economic content of Narodism and the criticism of it in Mr Struve's book*, 1894. In: Lenin's *Collected Works*, Progress Publishers, 1972. Volume 1 pages 333-508
[6] Karl Marx, *Critique of the Gotha Programme*, 1875.
[7] Karl Marx, *Preface to Contribution to a Critique of Political Economy*, 1859.
[8] Lenin, *The Three Sources and Three Component Parts of Marxism*, 1913.
[9] Karl Marx, Friedrich Engels, *The Communist Party Manifesto*, 1848.
[10] Lenin, *The Three Sources and Three Component Parts of Marxism*, 1913.
[11] Ibid.
[12] Ibid.
[13] Karl Marx, Friedrich Engels, *The Communist Party Manifesto*, 1848.
[14] Ibid.
[15] Ibid.
[16] Karl Marx. In: *Neue Rheinische Zeitung*, January-February, 1850.
[17] Ibid.
[18] Ibid.
[19] Arrigo Cervetto, "*The times of the Pacific Ocean*". In: *The Difficult Question of Times*, Marxist Science Publications, 2003.
[20] Karl Marx, Friedrich Engels, *The Communist Party Manifesto*, 1848.
[21] Piermaria Davoli, "Un miliardo e mezzo di salariati (*One and a half billion wage-earners*)". In: *Lotta Comunista* No. 454 June 2008.
[22] Karl Marx, Friedrich Engels, *The Communist Party Manifesto*, 1848.
[23] Karl Marx, *Capital*, Vol. 3.
[24] Lenin, *The Three Sources and Three Component Parts of Marxism*, 1913.
[25] Ibid.
[26] Arrigo Cervetto, "Le S.M.E tra dollaro e yen (*The S.M.E between the dollar and the Yen*)". In: *Imperialismo Unitario* (*Unitary Imperialism*) Lotta Comunista Editions, 1981
[27] Friedrich Engels, "Introduction" to: *In Memory of the German Blood-and-Thunder Patriots of 1806-1807*. Pamphlet No. XXIV of the Social-Democratic Library, published in Göttingen-Zurich in 1888.

[28] Arrigo Cervetto, "Il ciclo periodico del mutamento (*The periodic cycle of change*)". In: *Forze e forme del mutamento italiano* (*The forces and forms of change in Italy*), Lotta Comunista Editions, 1997.

[29] Lenin, *Prophetic Words.* Delivered 29th June 1918. First published 2nd July 1918, Pravda, No. 133 and signed N. Lenin. Published according to the Pravda text source: Lenin, *Collected Works*, 4th English edition, Progress Publishers, Moscow, 1972, Volume 27, pages 494-499. Translated: Clement Dutt: Edited by Robert Dalglish. Transcription/HTML Markup: David Walters and Robert Cymbala. Online Version: *Lenin Internet Archive* March 2002.

[30] Lenin, *Imperialism, the supreme phase of capitalism*, 1916.

[31] Ibid.

[32] Ibid.

[33] Guido la Barbera, "Crisi generale e secolo imperialista (*Widespread crisis and the imperialist century*)". In: *L'Europa e lo Stato* (*Europe and the state*), Lotta Comunista Editions February 1999.

[34] "Scienza marxista e teoria dell'imperialismo unitario *(Marxist science and the theory of unitary imperialism*)". In: *Lotta Comunista*, No. 438, February 2007

[35] Arrigo Cervetto, "La vera spartizione del mondo tra URSS e USA (*The real USSR-USA world partition*)". In: *L'imperialismo unitario (Unitary Imperialism)*, Lotta Comunista Editions 1981.

[36] Arrigo Cervetto, "Trionfo mondiale dell'instabile capitalismo (*World triumph of unstable capitalism*)". In: *Lotta Comunista*, No. 278, October 1993.

[37] Renato Pastorino, "Internationalism and the Unprecedented Task". In: *Bulletin Internationalist* No. 1 January 2002

[38] Paul Frölich, *War and politics in Germany 1914-1918.*

[39] Ibid.

[40] Ibid.

[41] Lenin, *The position and tasks of the Second International.* In: Lenin, *Collected Works*, Volume 21.

[42] Lenin, *The collapse of the Socialist International.* Ibid.

[43] Lenin, *The slogan of civil war illustrated.* Ibid.

[44] Lenin, *The collapse of the Second International.* Ibid.

[45] Lenin, Ibid.

[46] Roberto Casella, "Una pagina tenuto nascosta: l'opposizione in Germania al nazismo (*A hidden page: the opposition to Nazism in Germany*)". In: *Battaglie e principi per una politica comunista (Battles and principles for a Communist politics)*, Lotta Comunista Editions 1981.

[47] Ibid.

[48] "La pagina nascosta della Resistenza tedesca *(The German Resistance: a hidden page of history*)". In: *Lotta Comunista*, No. 451, March 2008.

[49] Ibid.

[50] Arrigo Cervetto, "The long capitalist development". In: *The difficult question of times,* Marxist Science Publications, 2003.

[51] Mario Silvestri, *The decay of Western Europe*, Einaudi, 1982.

52 "Organizzare la distruzione (*Organising Destruction*)". In: *Lotta Comunista*, No. 347-348 July-August 1999.

53 Ibid.

54 Arrigo Cervetto, "Riappare il fantasma di Yalta nella Polonia della nuova contesa (*The ghost of Yalta returns in fresh Polish conflict*)". In: *La Contesa Mondiale (World Contest*). Lotta Comunista Editions 1990.

55 Ibid.

56 Giovanni Poggi, "Le schede bianche e la crisi del parlamentarismo (*Spoiled voting papers and the crisis of parliamentarianism*)". In: *Lotta Comunista*, No. 10, December 1966.

57 Arrigo Cervetto, "Imperialist democracy". In: *The Political Shell*, Marxist Science Publications, 2006.

58 *Lenin, Imperialism and the split in socialism*. In: *Collected Works*, Volume 23, 1916.

59 Arrigo Cervetto, "La mezza guerra del Golfo (*The partial war in the Gulf*)". In: *Il Mondo Multipolare (The Multipolar World)*, Lotta Comunista Editions 1996.

60 Ibid.

61 Guido La Barbera, "Monete e missili (*Money and missile*)". In: *L'instabile ordine del moltipolarismo* (*Multipolarism's unstable world order*), Lotta Comunista Editions 2002.

62 Guido La Barbera, "Trasformazione euro-atlantica (*Euro-Atlantic Transformation*)". In: *L'instabile ordine del multipolarismo* (*Multipolarism's unstable world order*), Lotta Comunista Editions 2002.

63 Guido La Barbera, *L'Europa, L'Asia e la crisi* (*Europe, Asia and the crisis*), Lotta Comunista Editions 2008.

64 "A declining Washington in the new strategic phase". In: *Bulletin Internationalist* No. 82 October 2008.

65 Ibid.

66 "Exceptional powers and the world crisis". In: *Bulletin Internationalist* No. 82 October 2008.

67 "Europe and the State". In: *Bulletin Internationalist* No. 31 July 2004.

68 Ibid.

69 Arrigo Cervetto, "Il corso dell'imperialismo nel 1977-78 (*The course of imperialism 1977-78*)". In: *Imperialismo unitario* (*Unitary Imperialism*), Lotta Comunista Editions 1981.

70 "The global economy and the crisis". In: *Bulletin Internationalist* No. 75 March 2008.

71 Karl Marx, *Capital*. Book 3.

72 Julien Bouissou, "The IKEA system". In: *Le Monde* 30th August 2007.

73 "Panic on Wall Street". In: *Bulletin Internationalist* No. 82 October 2008.

74 J.W. Gilbart, *The History and principles of banking*. London, 1834, mentioned by Karl Marx, *Capital*, Book 3.

75 "The financial Tower of Babel collapses floor by floor". In: *Bulletin Internationalist* No. 78 June 2008.

[76] Guido La Barbera, "Le cifre politiche della bolla immobiliare (*The political figures of the house price bubble*)" In: *Lotta Comunista*, No. 422, October 2005.

[77] "The central bankers' August cannons". In: *Bulletin Internationalist* No. 69 September 2007.

[78] "House of cards of fictitious capital buffeted by housing bubble". In: *Bulletin Internationalist* No. 69, September 2007.

[79] "Panic on Wall Street". In: *Bulletin Internationalist* No. 82 October 2008.

[80] "A memorable storm". In: *Bulletin Internationalist* No. 82 October 2008.

[81] "Panic on Wall Street". In: *Bulletin Internationalist* No. 82 October 2008.

[82] Ibid.

[83] "A declining Washington in the new strategic phase". In: *Bulletin Internationalist* No. 82 October 2008.

[84] Massimo Gaggi, "Cereal Wars". In: *Corriere della Sera* 14th April 2008.

[85] "The political figures of the food crisis". In: *Bulletin Internationalist* No. 79 July 2008.

[86] "Inflation 'ready to serve'". In: *Bulletin Internationalist* No. 74 February 2008.

[87] "The political figures of the food crisis". In: *Bulletin Internationalist* No. 79 July 2008.

[88] "The social consequences of the crisis". In: *Bulletin Internationalist* No. 80 August 2008.

[89] "An opportunity for revolutionary clarity". In: *Bulletin Internationalist* No. 76 April 2008.

[90] Arrigo Cervetto, "Immigrati e donne nel welfare liberista (*Immigrants, women, and liberist welfare*)". In: *Il Mondo Multipolare* (*The Multipolar World*), Lotta Comunista Editions 1996.

[91] Piermaria Davoli, "Migrazioni gigantesche in Cina (*Gigantic migrations in China*)". In: *La classe operaia nel mondo 1975-2002* (*The working class in the world 1975-2002*), Lotta Comunista Editions 2003.

[92] Piermaria Davoli, "Un miliardo e mezzo di salariati (*One and a half billion wage-earners*)". In: *Lotta Comunista* No. 454 June 2008.

[93] Ibid.

[94] Karl Marx, Friedrich Engels, *The Communist Party Manifesto*.

[95] Ibid.

[96] Renato Pastorino, "A patient and persevering task". In: *Bulletin Internationalist* No. 65 May 2007.

[97] "The concrete sense of opposition to war". In: *Bulletin Internationalist* No. 13 January 2003.

[98] Ibid.

[99] Leon Trotsky. In: *The Difficult Question of Times*, Arrigo Cervetto. Marxist Science Publications 2003.

[100] Ibid.

[101] Lenin, *Imperialism, the supreme phase of capitalism.*

[102] Ibid.

[103] William Gumede, "China in Africa like the Marshall Plan". In: *Corriere della Sera* 28th April 2008.

[104] Roberto Casella, "Terremoto in Sichuan e 'sogno cinese' in Africa (*The Sezchuan earthquake and the "Chinese dream" in Africa*)". In: *Lotta Comunista* No. 454 June 2008.

[105] Ian Buruma, "Regime could turn aggressive if Chinese run stumbles". In: *Corriere della Sera* 27th December 2007.

[106] Guido La Barbera, *L'Europa e la guerra* (*Europe and the war*). Lotta Comunista Editions 2003.

[107] Lenin, "Fourth Anniversary of the October Revolution". In: *Collected Works* Volume 33.

[108] Hans Magnus Enzenberger, *Colloqui con Marx ed Engels* (*Conversations with Marx and Engels*). Einaudi Publishers 1977.

[109] Guido La Barbera, "Nello spazio i missili politici di Pechino (*Beijing's political missiles in space*)". In: *L'Europa, l'Asia e la crisi* (*Europe, Asia and the crisis*). Lotta Comunista Editions 2008.

[110] Leon Trotsky. In: *Le guerre balcaniche* (*The Balkan Wars 1912-1913*). Lotta Comunista Editions 1999.

[111] "Conscious opposition to new ideologies". In: *Bulletin Internationalist* No. 34 October 2004.

[112] Roberto Casella, "Mutazione imperialista del nazionalismo cinese (*Chinese nationalism's imperialist mutation*)". In: *Lotta Comunista* No. 453 May 2008.

[113] "Internationalism is the only policy for the future". In: *Bulletin Internationalist* No. 66 June 2007.

[114] Ibid.

[115] Ibid.

[116] "La scienza marxista contro le illusioni borghesi (*Marxist science versus bourgeois illusions*)". In: *Lotta Comunista* No. 447 November 2007.

[117] Roberto Casella "L'imbroglio ecologico (*The ecology tangle*)". In: *Battaglie e principi per una politica comunista* (*Battles and principles for a Communist politics*). Lotta Comunista Editions 2007.

[118] Renato Pastorino, "Certainties for a conscious struggle". In: *Bulletin Internationalist* No. 74 February 2008.

[119] Karl Marx, "Introduction" to: *Contribution to the critique of Hegel's Philosophy of Right* (1843).

[120] "A Communist politics to be defended and supported". In: *Bulletin Internationalist* No. 67 July 2007.

[121] "International struggle is the only hope and the only liberation". In: *Bulletin Internationalist* No. 79 July 2008.

[122] "Strikes in China". In: *Bulletin Internationalist* No. 73 January 2008.

[123] "Un orizzonte più ampio per la militanza di ogni giorno (*A wider horizon for daily militancy*)". In: *Bulletin Internationalist* No. 38 February 2005.

[124] Roberto Casella, "I sindacati dell'apatia aspettano un goveno amico (*Apathetic unions await a friendly government*)". In: *Lotta Comunista* No. 423 November 2005.

[125] "Continental powers and the world class". In: *Bulletin Internationalist* No. 44 August 2005.
[126] "Capitalist chaos, Communist conscience". In: *Bulletin Internationalist* N. 70 November 2007.
[127] Leon Trotsky. In: *Their morals and ours*, 1938.
[128] Renato Pastorino, "Il partito per l'epoca dell'imperialismo (*The party for the age of imperialism*)". In: *Bulletin Internationalist* No. 44 August 2005.
[129] Ibid.
[130] Ibid.
[131] Leon Trotsky. In: *Stalin*.
[132] Renato Pastorino, "The Bolshevik Model: Theory, Organization and Revolutionary Passion". In: *Bulletin Internationalist* N. 9 September 2002
[133] Renato Pastorino, "Il partito per l'epoca dell'imperialismo (*The party for the age of imperialism*)". In: *Bulletin Internationalist* No. 44 August 2005.
[134] Friedrich Engels, *Dialectics of Nature*. In: *Collected Works* of Marx and Engels Volume 25.
[135] Renato Pastorino, "I tempi del compito inedito (*The times of the unprecedented task*)". In: *Il compito inedito* (*The unprecedented task*). Lotta Comunista Editions 2006.
[136] Lenin, "Tasks of the Youth Leagues". In: *Collected Works* Volume 31.
[137] Renato Pastorino, "La profezia scientifica del Manifesto (*The Manifesto's scientific prophecy*)". In: *Lotta Comunista* No. 438 February 2007.
[138] Lenin, "Fear of the collapse of the old and the fight for the new". In: *Collected Works* Volume 26.

Book list of
ÉDITIONS SCIENCE MARXISTE
MARXIST SCIENCE PUBLICATIONS

English

Arrigo Cervetto — CLASS STRUGGLES AND THE REVOLUTIONARY PARTY
2000, 160 pages, paperback, $ 11 or £ 6.6
ISBN 2-912639-06-9

Arrigo Cervetto — THE DIFFICULT QUESTION OF TIMES
2003, 160 pages, paperback, $ 11 or £ 6,6
ISBN 2-912639-08-5

Arrigo Cervetto — THE POLITICAL SHELL
2006, 304 pages, paperback, $ 18 or £ 10
ISBN 2-912639-16-6

***** — THE COMMUNIST CHOICE
Understanding the Present, Changing the Future
2009, 144 pages, paperback, $ 7,00 or £ 4,50
ISBN 978-2-912639-37-0

Français

Collection Textes

Arrigo Cervetto — LA DIFFICILE QUESTION DES TEMPS
1997, 176 pages, br., € 11,00
Repères biographiques des noms cités
ISBN 2-912639-00-X

Arrigo Cervetto — LUTTES DE CLASSE ET PARTI RÉVOLUTIONNAIRE
1998, 160 pages, br., € 11,00
Repères biographiques des noms cités
ISBN 2-912639-01-8

Arrigo Cervetto — LE MONDE MULTIPOLAIRE 1990-1995
1998, 320 pages, br., € 17,00
21 cartes dans le texte, repères biographiques, index des idées, chronologie 1990-1995
ISBN 2-912639-02-6

Arrigo Cervetto — L'ENVELOPPE POLITIQUE
2008, 336 pages, br., € 15,00
index des noms, bibliographie
ISBN 978-2-912639-05-9

Guido La Barbera LA CRISE DU CAPITALISME D'ÉTAT
Écroulement d'un faux socialisme 1989-1995
1999, 512 pages, br., € 20,00
29 cartes, repères biographiques, chronologie 1989-1996, bibliographie
ISBN 2-912639-03-4

Guido La Barbera L'EUROPE ET LA GUERRE
2003, 336 pages, br., € 15,00
5 cartes, repères biographiques, chronologie 2000-2003
ISBN 2-912639-11-5

Guido La Barbera L'ORDRE INSTABLE DU MULTIPOLARISME
2004, 448 pages, br., € 17,00
9 cartes, repères biographiques, chronologie 1995-2001, bibliographie
ISBN 2-912639-12-3

Guido La Barbera L'EUROPE ET L'ÉTAT
2008, 288 pages, br., € 10,00
Index des noms, bibliographie
ISBN 978-2-912639-27-1

Guido La Barbera L'EUROPE, L'ASIE ET LA CRISE
2009, 512 pages, br., € 20,00
Chronologie 2003-2007, bibliographie, repères biographiques des noms cités
ISBN 978-2-912639-28-8

Renato Pastorino LA TÂCHE INÉDITE
2007, 224 pages, br., € 10,00
Index des noms, bibliographie
ISBN 978-2-912639-24-0

Collection Classiques

Karl Marx - Friedrich Engels
MANIFESTE DU PARTI COMMUNISTE
En appendice notes sur les premières éditions du *Manifeste* et sur sa diffusion
1999, 576 pages, cart., € 15,00
79 illustrations, repères biographiques, chronologie
ISBN 2-912639-04-2

Lev Trotsky — LES GUERRES BALKANIQUES 1912-1913
2002, 544 pages, br., € 23,00
6 cartes et 15 pages d'illustrations, glossaire, repères biographiques, répertoire des lieux, chronologie
ISBN 2-912639-10-7

Friedrich Engels — NOTES SUR LA GUERRE FRANCO-ALLEMANDE DE 1870-1871
Préface de Lev Trotsky
2008, 416 pages, cart., € 30,00
6 cartes hors texte et 13 cartes dans le texte ; 33 pages d'illustrations ; chronologie, index des noms, repères biographiques des noms cités
ISBN 978-2-912639-30-1

Collection Documents

G. Munis — LEÇONS D'UNE DÉFAITE, PROMESSE DE VICTOIRE
Critique et théorie de la révolution espagnole 1930-1939
2007, 640 pages, br., € 15,00
17 pages d'illustrations, 9 cartes ; chronologie, repères biographiques des noms cités
ISBN 978-2-912639-23-3

Collection Analyses

Nicola Capelluto – Franco Palumberi
ÉNERGIE ET PÉTROLE DANS L'AFFRONTEMENT IMPÉRIALISTE
2007, 320 pages, br., € 15,00
9 cartes et 47 tableaux statistiques, nombreux index
ISBN 978-2-912639-26-4

bibliothèque jeunes

Lénine — QUE FAIRE ?
Cervetto — La lutte décisive
2004, 352 pages, br., index des noms, € 5,00
ISSN 1772-4511 – ISBN 2-912639-13-1

Lénine	L'IMPÉRIALISME, STADE SUPRÊME DU CAPITALISME
Cervetto	La théorie marxiste des relations internationales
	2005, 192 pages, br., index des noms, € 5,00
	ISSN 1772-4511 – ISBN 2-912639-15-8
Cervetto	LÉNINE ET LA RÉVOLUTION CHINOISE
Lénine	« Matières inflammables de la politique mondiale » et autres écrits
	2006, 160 pages, br., index des noms, € 5,00
	ISSN 1772-4511 – ISBN 2-912639-19-0
Lénine	L'ÉTAT ET LA RÉVOLUTION
Cervetto	La restauration de la théorie marxiste
	2006, 192 pages, br., index des noms, € 5,00
	ISSN 1772-4511 – ISBN 978-2-912639-22-6
Lénine	LA MALADIE INFANTILE DU COMMUNISME (LE « COMMUNISME DE GAUCHE »)
Cervetto	Le temps de la clarté de Lénine
	2007, 192 pages, br., index des noms, € 5,00
	ISSN 1772-4511 – ISBN 978-2-912639-17-2
Engels	ANTIDÜHRING
Cervetto	La découverte de la politique
	2007, 448 pages, br., index des noms, € 5,00
	ISSN 1772-4511 – ISBN 978-2-912639-25-7
Marx – Engels	LA CONCEPTION MATÉRIALISTE DE L'HISTOIRE
	Anthologie
Cervetto	Les temps de la science de la révolution
	2008, 192 pages, br., index des noms, € 5,00
	ISSN 1772-4511 – ISBN 978-2-912639-29-5
Marx	LA GUERRE CIVILE EN FRANCE
Cervetto	La forme politique enfin découverte
	2008, 160 pages, br., index des noms, € 5,00
	ISSN 1772-4511 – ISBN 978-2-912639-31-8
Lénine	MATÉRIALISME ET EMPIRIOCRITICISME
	Notes critiques sur une philosophie réactionnaire
Cervetto	La critique libérale de Bernstein
	2009, 448 pages, br., index des noms, € 7,00
	ISSN 1772-4511 – ISBN 978-2-912639-34-9
****	LE CHOIX COMMUNISTE
	Comprendre le présent, changer l'avenir
	2009, 160 pages, br., € 5,00
	ISSN 1772-4511 – ISBN 978-2-912639-33-2

Allemand

Arrigo Cervetto KLASSENKÄMPFE UND REVOLUTIONÄRE PARTEI
2000, 176 pages, br., € 11,00
ISBN 2-912639-07-7

Arrigo Cervetto DIE POLITISCHE HÜLLE (L'enveloppe politique)
2003, 320 pages, br., € 15,00
ISBN 2-912639-09-3

Espagnol

Arrigo Cervetto LUCHA DE CLASES Y PARTIDO REVOLUCIONARIO
2006, 192 pages, br., € 10,00
ISBN 2-912639-20-4

Éditions russes

(Éditions Science Marxiste
en collaboration avec les Éditions Prometey de Saint-Pétersbourg)

Arrigo Cervetto UNITARNII IMPERIALISM, tom I
(L'impérialisme unitaire, tome I)
2005, 796 pages, cart., 250 roubles
18 cartes dans le texte, index, repères biographiques, notes
ISBN 2-912639-14-X

Arrigo Cervetto UNITARNII IMPERIALISM, tom II
(L'impérialisme unitaire, tome II)
2005, 736 pages, cart., 250 roubles
21 cartes dans le texte, index, repères biographiques, notes
ISBN 2-912639-18-2

Arrigo Cervetto MNOGOPOLIARNI MIR 1990-1995
(Le monde multipolaire)
2006, 350 pages, cart., 250 roubles
21 cartes dans le texte, index, repères biographiques
ISBN 2-912639-21-2

Arrigo Cervetto KLASSOVAIA BOR'BÁ I REVOLIUTSIONNAIA PARTIA
(Luttes de classe et parti révolutionnaire)
2000, 160 pages, br., 25 roubles
ISBN 5-901606-01-9
(Éditions Praxis, Moscou, sur licence Éditions Science Marxiste)

Éditions NOVY PROMETEY

Saint-Pétersbourg – Russie

Arrigo Cervetto	TRUDNIY VOPROS VREMENI (La difficile question des temps) 2007, 160 pages, index, cart., 175 roubles ISBN 978-5-91258-033-8
Vladimir Nevski	ISTORA RKP(B). KRATIJ OCHERK (Histoire du Parti Communiste russe (bolchevik) 2009, 804 pages, cart., 450 roubles En appendice biographie et deux essais de l'Auteur 9 cartes, 77 illustrations, notes, chronologie, bibliographie, repères biographiques ISBN 978-5-9901606-1-3
Anthologie	OBRAZOVANIE KOMMUNISTICHESKOGO INTERNAZIONALA. MART 1919 GODA (Fondation de l'Internationale Communiste. Mars 1919) 2009, 152 pages, br., 120 roubles Chronologie, repères biographiques ISBN 978-5-9901606-2-0

Éditions brésiliennes
Edições INTERVENÇÃO COMUNISTA

Niterói-RJ. – Brésil

Arrigo Cervetto	LUTAS DE CLASE E PARTIDO REVOLUCIONÁRIO (Luttes de classe et parti révolutionnaire) 2007, 176 pages, br.
Arrigo Cervetto	LÊNIN E A REVOLUÇAO CHINESA (Lénine et la révolution chinoise)
Lénine	« Material inflamável na politica mundial » e outros textos 2008, 160 pages, br.
*****	A ESCOLHA COMUNISTA (Le choix communiste) 2009, 160 pages, br.

Éditions grecques
εκδόσεις ΔΙΕΘΝΙΣΜΟΣ
Éditions DIETHNISMOS (Internationalisme)

Pirée – Grèce

Anthologie	Ο ΜΥΘΟΣ ΤΟΥ ΚΑΛΠΙΚΟΥ ΣΟΣΙΑΛΙΣΜΟΥ (Le mythe du socialisme faux) 318 pages, broché, € 9,00
Arrigo Cervetto	ΤΑΞΙΚΟΙ ΑΓΩΝΕΣ ΚΑΙ ΕΠΑΝΑΣΤΑΤΙΚΟ ΚΟΜΜΑ (Luttes de classe et parti révolutionnaire) 205 pages, broché, € 9,00
Arrigo Cervetto	ΤΟ ΔΥΣΚΟΛΟ ΖΗΤΗΜΑ ΤΩΝ ΧΡΟΝΩΝ (La difficile question des temps) 160 pages, relié, € 9,00

Printed in June 2009
by *Galli Thierry Stampa s.r.l.*
Milan, Italy

Constitution
uncertainty is not the excuse for
indeterminations

let fear to undermine the (iron) nation
stir up (steel)s.
unrest(?)

Communism – emergency